MAKING AND REPAIRING
◈ WOODEN ◈
CLOCK CASES

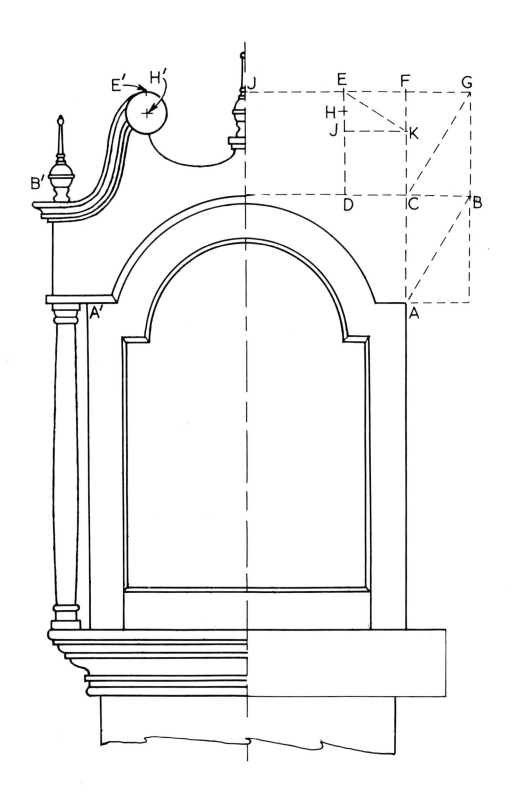

MAKING AND REPAIRING
◇ WOODEN ◇
CLOCK CASES

V.J. Taylor & H.A. Babb

David & Charles

A DAVID & CHARLES BOOK

First published in the UK in 1986
Reprinted 1987, 1991, 1994

First published in paperback 1994
Reprinted 2002

Distributed in North America
by F&W Publications, Inc.
4700 E. Galbraith Rd.
Cincinnati, OH 45236
1-800-289-0963

A catalogue record for this book is available from the
British Library.

ISBN 0 7153 0286 8 (paperback)

Typeset by Typesetters (Birmingham) Limited
and printed in England by Butler & Tanner Ltd
for David & Charles
Brunel House   Newton Abbot   Devon

Contents

Dedicated to our respective wives for their
patience, forebearance, and much typing!

Preface

Many excellent books have been written about antique and modern clocks. Although these give comprehensive coverage of makers, designs, and every type of movement, both for making and repairing, none as yet seems to represent a serious attempt to cover the making and repairing of clock cases. It is hoped that this book will fill the gap.

It must be stressed here that repairing is very different from restoring and nothing described in this book is to be regarded as restoration work, which is a job for the skilled craftsman. Generally speaking, repair work is done to correct structural faults in the case so that it may continue to enclose the movement and keep it working. Restoration carries on from the repair stage to restore the case to its original state as far as this can be ascertained; this has been to some extent covered in other publications. A fuller outline of the principles of restoration and conservation is given in Appendix I.

This book aims to provide information on every aspect of repair work and to explain the processes involved in the making and designing of various types of cases, though for reasons of space some less well-known and less popular types cannot be included.

Introduction

When writing a book of this kind it is necessary to decide what level of woodworking skills the reader is likely to have achieved. The only way to circumvent this is to start from basics and describe the whole range of woodworking techniques before starting on the real subject of the book.

We have therefore assumed that the reader is a serious amateur woodworker who has a thorough mastery of standard practices in cabinet making and polishing. It is inadvisable for the complete novice to attempt the type of work dealt with here.

Assuming that you have a place to work and a suitable bench, the following tools should prove useful: hammer (the London pattern is best); mallet; panel saw; crosscut saw; tenon saw, 305mm (12in) with 12 or 14 points per 25mm (1in); dovetail saw, 203mm (8in) with 18 to 22 points per 25mm (1in); coping saw; smoothing plane, 229mm (9in) long; jack plane (optional) 407mm (16in) long; block plane; metal rabbet or fillister plane; firmer chisels, one each 25, 12 and 6mm (1in, ½in, and ¼in); bevelled-edge chisels (optional) in the same sizes; 12mm and 6mm (½in and ¼in) mortise chisels; one firmer and one scribing gouge, both 12mm (½in); brace and accompanying bits for holes 6mm (¼in) diameter and upwards; hand drill and accompanying drills for holes up to 6mm (¼in) diameter; bradawl; try square; folding or retracting rule; mitre square; marking gauge; set of punches; set of screwdrivers; pincers; rasp; metal spokeshave; oil stones and slips (for gouges); cabinet scraper; steel straight-edge; craft knife with spare blades.

This list looks formidable, but you may already have many of the items as they are normal household DIY tools. Of course, if you have some power tools and a router you can dispense with many of the hand tools, and a motorised saw-bench will reduce the number even more.

To enable readers to find information quickly, the book has been divided into sections. Thus, Section 1 deals with problems of repairs to doors, joints, panels, mouldings, veneers, marquetry, inlays, bandings, ormolu, boulle, lacquer work, polishes and finishes, and gilding.

Section 2 describes how to design longcase clocks, bracket clocks, Vienna regulators, tavern and mural clocks, balloon clocks, and hooded clocks, and then continues with full details of construction for each design.

Section 3 is concerned with workshop techniques and projects such as workshop geometry, making fielded panels, split turnings, decorative veneering, moulding designs, making inverted bell-tops, making circular frames, making fluted and twist columns, pelleting, and fixing glass.

There are also three appendices giving detailed information on conservation, the properties of adhesives, and wood-boring insects. Other useful items are a glossary of British/American equivalent terms, and a list of suppliers of specialist materials.

1 Repairs to Doors, Joints and Panels

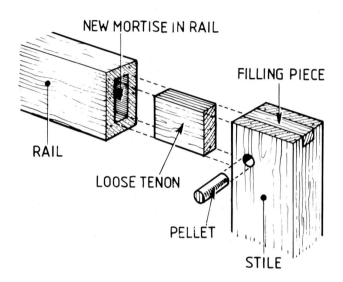

NEW MORTISE IN RAIL

FILLING PIECE

RAIL

LOOSE TENON

PELLET

STILE

This chapter deals comprehensively with the various repair jobs you are likely to encounter and the best ways to approach them; they are just as applicable to furniture in general as to clock cases in particular. As emphasised in the introduction to this book, we presuppose that you have a good knowledge of basic woodwork, and a kit of tools to go with it. In addition to the woodworking tools already listed, you need an assortment of cramping devices, plus a sharp craft knife or two, and these will be described as we go along. Each problem appears under its own heading for easy reference.

◇ DOORS 'IN WIND' ◇

This is a common, annoying and difficult problem to solve as each case has to be dealt with individually. Basically it is due to the wood of the frame having twisted in its length (Fig 1), either in the whole of its length or in one localised area. It is just the kind of fault which would occur, say, with a regulator clock case door and it could, of course, lead to the glass cracking, among other troubles.

If the door is a new one, the hard way is usually the most effective and this means dismantling the frame and replacing the twisted pieces. Another method is to cramp the stile into the reverse direction and leave it as long as possible in the cramps, or to achieve the same result by leaving it under a heavy weight; but although it may be straight when first released from the cramps, it is likely to resume its former curvature after a short time owing to the inherent structure of the grain. It is better to replace it.

If dealing with an old door from an existing clock case, you have to decide whether or not you can dismantle the frame. If dismantling is impossible, try the method shown in Fig 2. Here, the offending part is cramped to a bench and a series of saw-kerfs is made across it; wedge-shaped pieces of hardwood are tapped into these kerfs and, by trial and error, the cramps are released to see if the piece remains straight; if not, the wedges are tapped in a little more until it does. Then the wedges are taken out, glued and reinserted; once the glue has set they can be carefully chiselled down flush.

This procedure is suitable only for the inside of a door because no matter how well you stain and polish the ends of the wedges, they are bound to show as their grain will be at right angles to that of the stile. However, if you are dealing with a veneered door frame, then you may be in luck, as it is normally not too difficult to remove the veneer, kerf-and-wedge as described above, and then relay the veneer. All clock cases over fifty years old have almost certainly been glued up with the Scotch glue (including hide, bone, skin and fish glue) that was used before modern synthetic adhesives were invented, and this can

be softened easily by warming with a hair-dryer or by holding a rag dampened in hot water against the veneer. A point to note when kerfing is that each cut tends to make a kink or bump on the opposite side, so rather than relying on one or two fairly deep kerfs it is better to have several shallow ones close together.

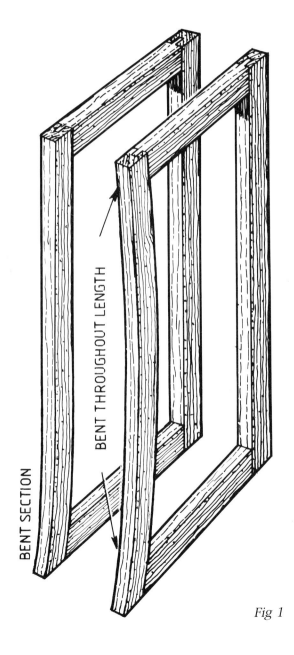

BENT THROUGHOUT LENGTH

BENT SECTION

Fig 1

The last example relates to the specific circumstances where the curve is localised at one end, towards the corner, and when the frame can be dismantled. The method of repair is shown in Fig 3. This involves making a cut on each side of the mortise and to the full depth of the stile, and continuing it for two or three inches beyond the mortise. A practised hand could probably do this with a tenon saw, but you may find it easier to use a machine. The next step is to make up some hardwood slips of the same width as the stile and the same thickness as the saw-cuts and glue them in; then cramp the assembly flat and allow the glue to set. Do not be tempted to make one saw-cut down the centre as this would mean that the hardwood slip in the mortise would have to be cut away to allow the tenon to enter.

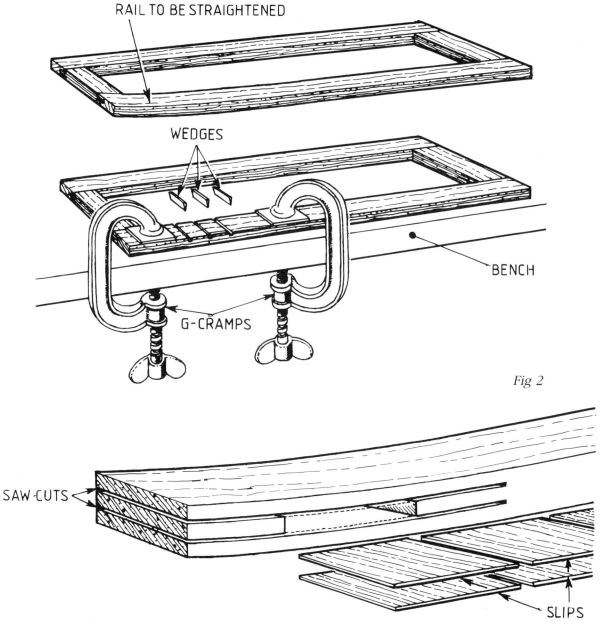

RAIL TO BE STRAIGHTENED

WEDGES

G-CRAMPS

BENCH

Fig 2

SAW CUTS

SLIPS

Fig 3

◇ JOINTS ◇

One of the most frequent faults is when a joint on a panelled door has opened, usually because of the pressure exerted by a panel splitting (Fig 4), but sometimes because the glue has perished.

If the joint is at the corner of a panelled frame, the first thing to do is to find out if the panel is loose, as it should be. In the years before plywood and other man-made boards, such panels were of solid wood and in anticipation of the tricks that solid timber can play, old-time craftsmen left them loose in grooves in the framing rails so that the panels could swell or shrink to a reasonable extent. So hold one stile of the frame in a vice (using protective pads on the vice jaws) and then place your hands flat on either side of the panel to see if you can move it. If you cannot, then perhaps there is a moulding pinned to it and to the framing and this will have to come off along the side on which you are working. Or it may be that glue has spread from the joints and is holding the panel, and if so you will have to insert a thin-bladed knife and break the glue bond.

Before you knock the joint apart prior to regluing it, cut all round the joint with the tip of a sharp knife to break away any remaining glue and also to clean out the gap, and then use a mallet to tap the stile and rail apart. If all traces of old glue are not removed the new glue will not hold. The job is best done by wiping away the old Scotch glue with a rag dampened in hot water; you may need to scrape it away inside the mortise. Once the work has dried you can re-glue and cramp it up.

The split mortise (Fig 5) is another trouble which sometimes occurs and is usually the result of the door having been subjected to strain. In mild cases it is a matter of cleaning out the split (which, on old pieces, is probably half-filled with dust, furniture polish etc), removing all traces of the old glue and then regluing and cramping the joint. In bad cases, where the split has opened up and some of the wood is missing, you must separate the joint before you can make any progress. First of all, examine it carefully to check if there are any nails, screws, or wooden pins holding the joint together. Any such nails or

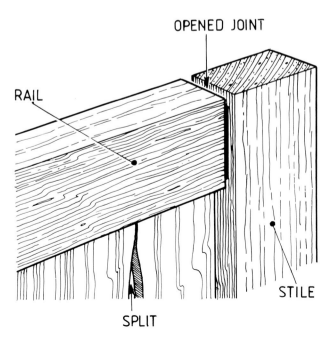

Fig 4

screws must be removed, of course; if there are wooden pins, drill them out with a drill of the same diameter. The separated parts will look like the illustration in Fig 6.

Obviously, the open split above the mortise will have to be filled, and it is best to tidy up the split by sawing cuts so that a filling piece can be glued in (Fig 7). If the tenon is too thin for the mortise, small pieces of veneer can be glued to the cheeks to make it fit better. If you are going to repin the joint you need to make holes in these veneer pieces for the pin.

One method of remaking the joint without pinning is shown in Fig 7. This assumes that the tenon which has a hole through it is replaced by a loose tenon – which will necessitate cutting a new mortise in the rail, as shown. The hole in the stile needs to be pelleted and the method of making pellets is described on page 160.

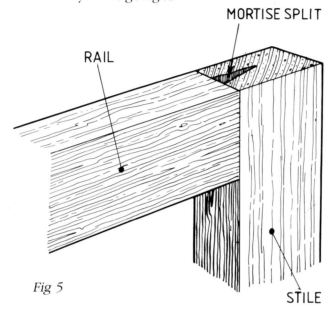

Fig 5

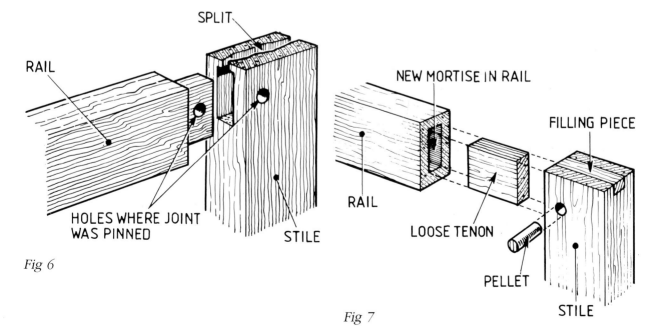

Fig 6

Fig 7

◇ SPLIT FRAMED PANELS ◇

This problem is almost always due to the fact that the panel is not free to move in the framing and when it shrinks a split is caused along the grain. The two most probable causes of a fixed panel are as explained under Joints, above, namely, either that nails or screws are holding it, or that some of the glue from a joint has accidentally spread on to it.

Both causes must be removed as you must be able to close the two pieces together once the edges of the split have been cleaned off and glued. Cleaning out the split can be troublesome and it is often necessary to chip off the old glue with the tip of a thin-bladed knife and then wipe the area with a rag dampened with hot water.

Figs 8 and 9 show two ways of cramping the split pieces together while the glue sets. The important consideration is whether or not it is possible to drive wood screws into the back of the panel, and if you can, then Fig 8 shows the method to adopt. If you cannot, things get more complicated and we suggest using cramps as in Fig 9. Here, ordinary G-cramps are fixed on the panel (with protective blocks) and then a sash cramp is arranged so that its jaws bear on the threads of the G-cramps. Alternatively, you can use battens instead of the protective blocks. These battens will have to be notched at the ends by the amount that the panel stands back from the frame; the set-up is shown in Fig 10. Work glue into the split with a thin sliver of veneer and wipe away any surplus glue with a wet cloth (this is the golden rule whenever you apply glue). One snag that can arise is that the two lips of the split do not go together exactly level and you only find this out after the glue has set and you have removed

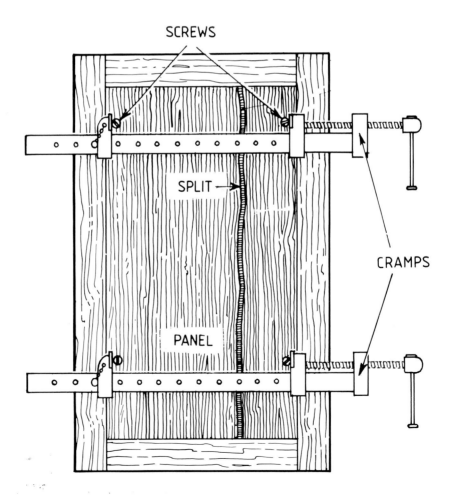

Fig 8

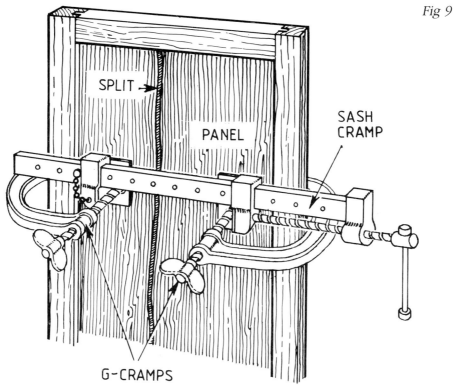

Fig 9

Fig 10

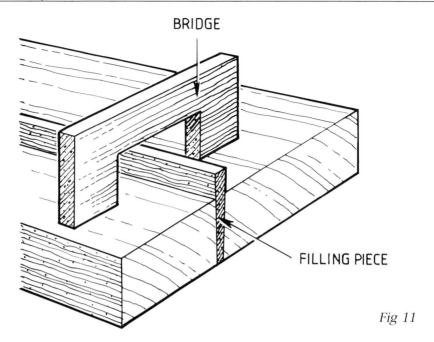

BRIDGE

FILLING PIECE

Fig 11

the cramps. A simple device to guard against this is illustrated in Fig 11 – a tiny bridge which will show up any inequality.

There is another type of panel split, however, which is caused by a natural shake developing, and in this case there would be no point in cramping the two parts together because the wood is inherently under stress and would soon separate again. A thin sliver of matching wood needs to be pressed into the gap as shown in Fig 12; it usually helps to open the split at its narrow end so that the width is the same throughout its length. The sliver, which should be slightly wedge-shaped in section, is glued in and any excess glue wiped off; then you should use the bridge referred to in Fig 11 to check the levels.

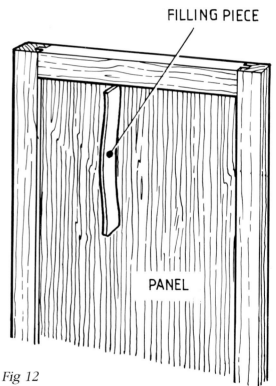

FILLING PIECE

PANEL

Fig 12

◇ SOLID PANELS ◇

So far we have considered putting right faults in framed-up panels, which are always comparatively thin – say 5mm (³⁄₁₆in) or 6mm (¼in). The thicker type of solid wood panels, such as those used for the sides of the trunk of a longcase clock, bring their own troubles.

Warping is sometimes a problem, and here it must be emphasised that the remedies proposed relate only to loose panels which can be handled on the bench. If a clock case has a warped panel there is nothing you can do about it without dismantling it first.

One recommendation is to damp the hollow side with clean, cold water and turn the panel upside down for a day or so. In our experience the panel resumes its hollow shape as the moisture dries out, so you have wasted your time! In any case, if the surface is waxed or varnished the water will not really penetrate the grain, and you will probably mark the finish and give yourself another job to do.

A rather drastic method (Fig 13) is to cut the panel into strips lengthwise, true up each edge with a plane or an overhand planer so that it is at right angles to the face, and then glue the strips together. You will need an extra strip to compensate for the wood lost in sawing and planing. Both sides will have to be veneered, as if you veneer only the show-face the piece will be pulled into a curve by the stretching of the veneer. However, this method cannot be recommended from the point of view of conservation, as it destroys the original appearance, so it should be confined to repair work only.

This tendency of a veneer to exert a pulling effect can be used to correct curvature or 'bowing'. The veneer is laid on the rounded or convex face (Fig 14), with the grain running in the same direction as that of the panels. The surface should be toothed before applying the veneer, which should be laid with a veneer hammer (see page 138) – the more the hammer is worked across the grain, and the more heat and moisture employed, the more pronounced will be the stretching of the veneer and the greater the pulling effect.

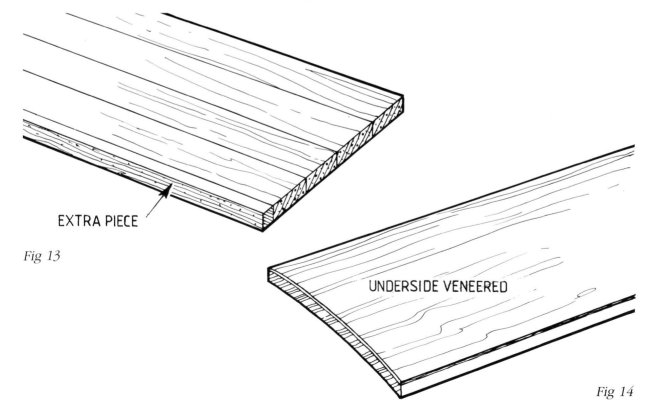

EXTRA PIECE

Fig 13

UNDERSIDE VENEERED

Fig 14

There is one more expedient you can try and, again, it is rather drastic; the necessary set-up is shown in Fig 15. A series of parallel saw-cuts is made on the hollow side of the panel, and the best way to do this is with a portable circular saw guided by battens cramped to the panel and moved across for each cut. If you try to cut them on a saw-bench, the curvature of the panel will cause the depths of the saw-cuts to differ, and the whole point is that they should be equal.

The depth of the saw-cuts is critical and needs to be up to two-thirds of the panel thickness; cuts that are too deep tend to produce a series of flats. Of equal importance is the distance between the cuts; it should be about 25mm (1in) – a wider distance tends to show signs of the bending.

Ideally, the panel should be supported on something like a pair of trestles so that each end projects; this will allow you to position two G-cramps, as shown, so that the panel is held between the two battens. Thin strips, slightly wedge-shaped in section, are tapped into the saw-cuts and stand a trifle proud so that you can plane them flush once the glue has set; the small blocks allow the batten to bridge across the protruding strips. The ends of the strips should be trimmed flush, and coloured to match the original panel.

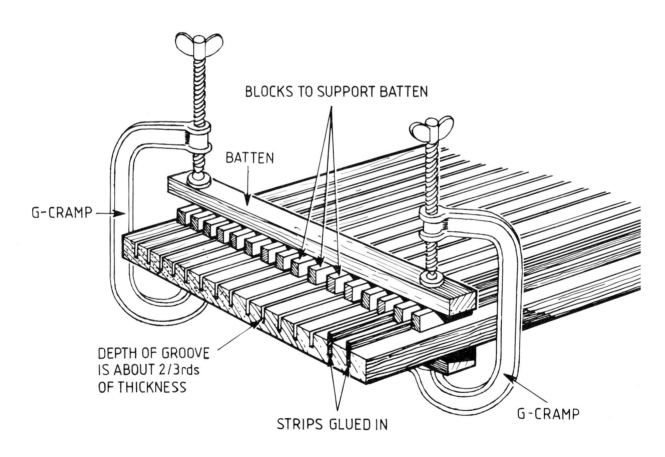

Fig 15

◇ WIDE SPLITS ◇

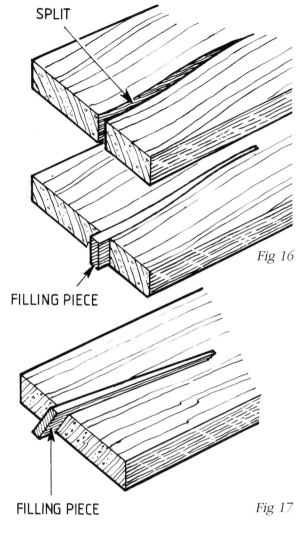

SPLIT

FILLING PIECE

Fig 16

This treatment is intended to fill a wide split which needs more than a sliver; a typical example would be an end shake, Fig 16. It is usually necessary to match grain as much as possible, so this determines the kind of wood used.

After scraping away all traces of old glue, polish, dirt, etc, open up the narrow end a little with a thin-bladed saw (a hacksaw blade is suitable); it is quite possible that the split is at an angle which follows the medullary rays and in such circumstances you must retain the angle while you are opening the split (Fig 17).

The filling piece should then be tapped in and glued, and the levels of the surfaces on either side of the split checked with the little bridging device mentioned under Split Framed Panels. Once the glue has set, the protruding edges of the filling piece can be flushed off. If you have any doubt about the result, you can insert a dovetail key (Figs 18A and B) once the glue has set. This key can either go right through or can be blind, depending on whether or not it can be seen.

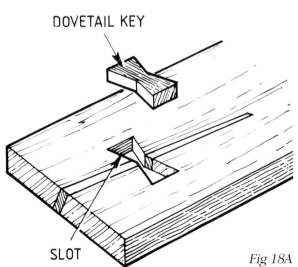

FILLING PIECE

Fig 17

DOVETAIL KEY

SLOT

Fig 18A

Fig 18B

◇ HINGES AND DOORS ◇

If the door has dropped, unscrew the hinge leaf which is fixed to the case and fit a piece of veneer into the recess (or use a piece of card) then refix the hinge; the same method can be used on the top hinge if the leaf has been fixed into a recess that is too deep – this kind of fault causes the door to bind along the top edge. If the door persists in springing open when you try to shut it, try putting a piece of veneer behind both top and bottom hinge leaves – this should cure the trouble. Take care not to use screws of too large a gauge for the hinges, as the screw heads will not fit into the countersunk holes and thus can give any of the symptoms described above. The counter-sinking in the leaves of the hinges can be enlarged to take larger screws, thus avoiding the need to plug the holes, but in the interests of conservation the method should be used only for repair, and not for restoration.

Fig 20

A similar problem exists when the wood has sheared away from the hinge screws (Fig 20). Once again, the hinge screws have to be withdrawn and then lines should be scored around the damage. The short lines are angled slightly to give a dovetailed effect which will prevent the repair patch from being pulled out again (Fig 21). Chisel away the damaged area to the scored lines and cut a piece of wood to fit; this is glued in and cramped, and once the glue has set it can be trimmed flush and new screw holes drilled.

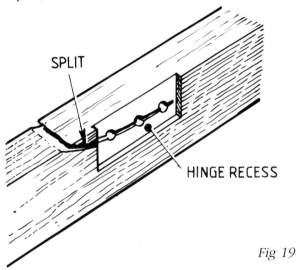

Fig 19

If a door has been subjected to heavy strain the result can be a split along the hinge (Fig 19). To mend this, remove the hinge leaf and prise open the split to remove any loose splinters or dust. Then fill the split with glue and rub some on the surface around it as well. Cramp the parts together with a G-cramp and protective blocks and, while the glue is still wet, push some tapered wooden plugs into the screw holes. When the glue has set the plugs can be trimmed flush and new holes drilled.

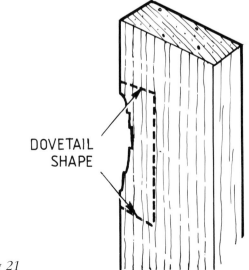

Fig 21

◇ BRUISES ◇

A bruise on solid wood which is not veneered can sometimes be taken out by laying a piece of damp cloth over it and applying a warm electric iron so that the heat and moisture will cause the wood to swell. If the bruise is a small one you can substitute a soldering iron for the electric one, but in either case take it gently and if the timber shows signs of turning red, stop immediately. Moisture will not enter a waxed or polished surface, of course, so in this case you can try pricking small holes over the area before starting the treatment.

Large bruises and dents may be so bad that the only course is to patch them. Cut the patch from a piece of matching wood and make it diamond-shaped to cover the dent comfortably; bevel the edges of the patch slightly (Fig 22A). Lay the patch over the dent so that the larger face is uppermost, and then score round the bottom edge with a marking knife; mark one end of the patch to coincide with a similar mark on the surface so that you know which way to fit it (Fig 22B).

Carefully cut out the wood from the diamond shape you have just marked and try the patch for size, trimming it to fit. If the surface is not polished, the patch can stand proud so that it can be planed flush when the glue has set; otherwise you will have to keep trying and trimming the patch until it fits perfectly. As the edges are bevelled it will need to be tapped gently into place with a mallet and protective block.

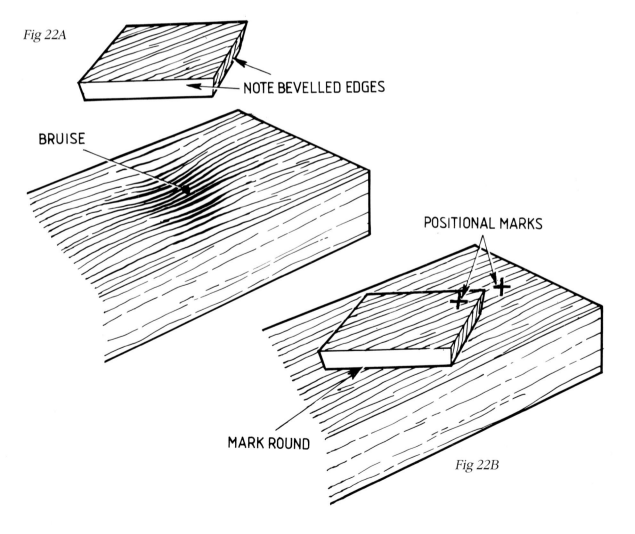

Fig 22A

NOTE BEVELLED EDGES

BRUISE

POSITIONAL MARKS

MARK ROUND

Fig 22B

◇ CUSTOM-BUILT CRAMPS ◇

In addition to the normal complement of workshop cramps such as sash cramps, G-cramps, hand screws, band cramps, and so on, you can improvise some for yourself. The following are a few suggestions (see Figs 23A–E):

(A) Pieces of tensioned wire cut from upholstery springs are very handy for small work, for instance holding a cocked bead into its grooves while the glue sets.

(B) The tourniquet or 'Spanish windlass' method. This consists of a loop of strong cord which encircles the work being cramped; a piece of dowel is caught through the loop and when it twists the cord it exerts a strong pressure.

(C) A more sophisticated development of the tourniquet principle which can be used on rectangular shapes. Tension is applied by turning the wing-nut: protective padding is needed at each corner.

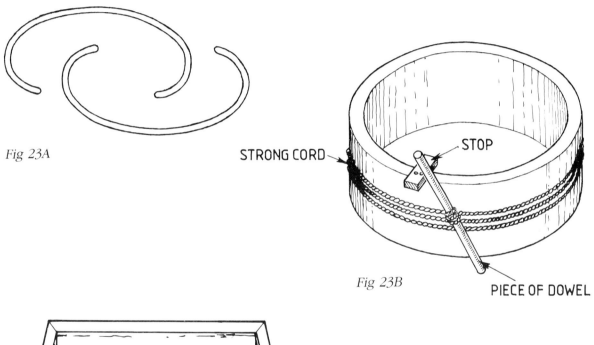

Fig 23A

STRONG CORD

STOP

Fig 23B

PIECE OF DOWEL

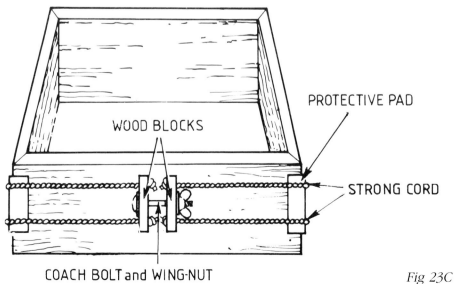

PROTECTIVE PAD

WOOD BLOCKS

STRONG CORD

COACH BOLT and WING-NUT

Fig 23C

(D) This is one of the most useful cramping gadgets and you could easily make it up as a permanent feature. The baseboard and fixed blocks should be more or less the same thickness (22mm/⅞in would be suitable) and the folding wedges should be half as long again as the width of the baseboard, and tapered at an angle of about 1 in 8. You could increase the usefulness of the device by arranging for the left-hand fixed block to be held by G-cramps instead of being screwed down, as this would enable you to vary the width to suit the work to be cramped.

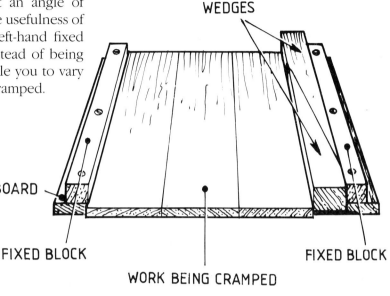

Fig 23D

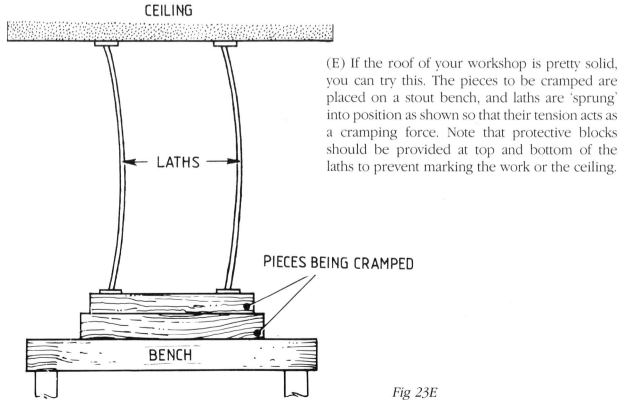

(E) If the roof of your workshop is pretty solid, you can try this. The pieces to be cramped are placed on a stout bench, and laths are 'sprung' into position as shown so that their tension acts as a cramping force. Note that protective blocks should be provided at top and bottom of the laths to prevent marking the work or the ceiling.

Fig 23E

2 Repairs to Mouldings

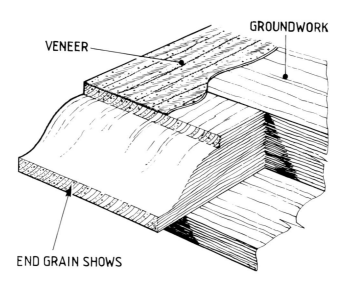

VENEER

GROUNDWORK

END GRAIN SHOWS

In this chapter we shall be discussing repairs to the various kinds of mouldings found on clock cases. The basic types of mouldings and beads are defined while some of the designs are described later, in Chapter 10.

There are three distinct types of mouldings, one of which is the 'stuck' moulding which is worked on the solid edge (see Fig 24A); another is the 'bolection' moulding which is worked separately and then rabbeted on to the job (Fig 24B). The third type is the 'composite' moulding which, as its name suggests, is built up separately and then glued (or glued and pinned) into place. It is built up with the moulded facing glued to a core of less expensive timber, which is often softwood (Fig 24C).

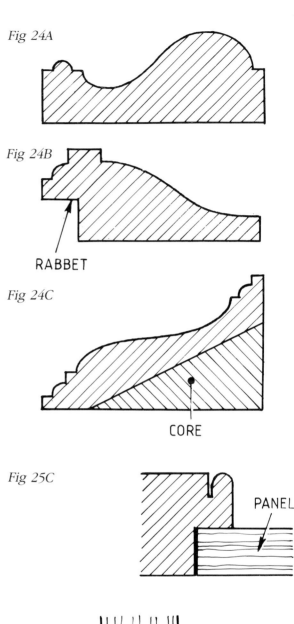

Fig 24A

Fig 24B

RABBET

Fig 24C

CORE

Strictly, a bead is a small semicircular moulding applied to an edge and can be known alternatively as a 'fillet' or an 'astragal' (Fig 25A). A 'cocked' bead (Fig 25B) is one which projects above the surrounding surface; 'bead and flush' refers to one which is worked and let in around a panel (Fig 25C); a 'bead and quirk' is a bead with a tiny groove sunk alongside it (Fig 25D); finally, there is the 'staff' or 'return' bead which is worked on a corner arris with a quirk on each side (Fig 25E) – it is often employed on a mitred corner so that if the joint opens the gap is less obtrusive. (An 'arris' describes more precisely than the word 'edge' the junction between one plane surface and another, usually but not necessarily at right angles to each other.)

Fig 25C

PANEL

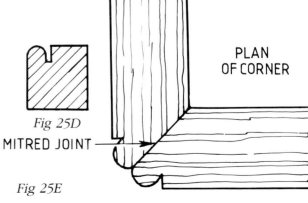

PLAN
OF CORNER

Fig 25D

MITRED JOINT

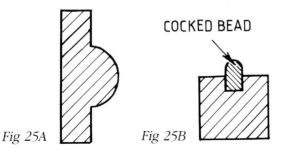

COCKED BEAD

Fig 25A   *Fig 25B*   *Fig 25E*

◇ STUCK MOULDINGS ◇

Fig 26A shows typical damage or bruising to a corner. There are two ways of dealing with it, depending on the position of the damage and whether or not the object is likely to be lifted by the moulding, as in the case of a bracket clock being moved carelessly.

Obviously, you need to use a matching piece for the repair. Having chosen it, lay it aside while you consider where to saw away the damage, Fig 26B. It is good practice to make the saw-cut not at right angles to the surfaces but at an angle as shown at Fig 26C so that a larger gluing area results – this is important because it is the glue alone which holds the filling piece on; the greater the gluing area, the better the result. The method of shaping the profile of the moulding is described under the heading 'Working Mouldings' later in this chapter.

Turning our attention now to more serious damage, we have illustrated the procedure in Figs 27A–C, so let us go through it step-by-step.

Assuming you have found a matching piece to use for the repair, cut away the damage as in Fig 27A, noting that the inner end is cut at an angle (approximately 45 degrees is suitable), and then clean the whole thing up. Offer up the filling piece as shown, making sure that it is about 6mm (¼in) oversize on the edges and about 3mm (⅛in) oversize in thickness. Hold the filling piece firmly in place and mark the centre line for the fixing dowel (which is inserted later) on to it and on to the surface being repaired.

Next, drill the holes for the dowel, but be careful to drill the one in the filling piece a trifle away from your marked line; the dotted line in Fig 27B shows the idea. The difference need only be 1mm (¹⁄₃₂in) or even less, but means that you can shave off the slanting edges to get a perfect fit. If you do not do the job this way you could finish with a filling piece which, when dowelled on, reveals a gap between the slanting faces which would involve plugging and re-drilling holes.

Fig 27C is a plan view and shows how the filling piece is cut oversize. If you have a similar problem on an edge which is quite plain and square you can adopt the same procedure, but as

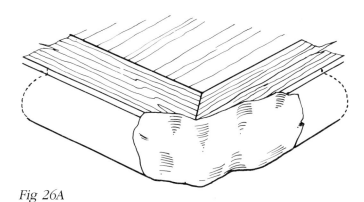

Fig 26A

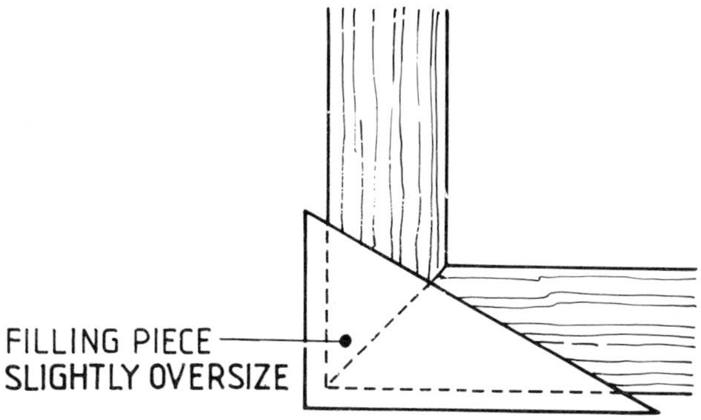

FILLING PIECE
SLIGHTLY OVERSIZE

Fig 26B (Plan)

ANGLED CUT GIVES LARGER GLUING AREA

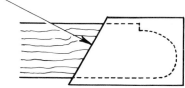

Fig 26C

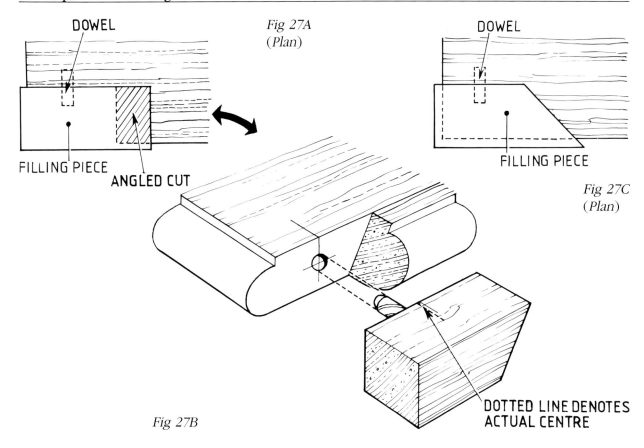

DOWEL

FILLING PIECE   ANGLED CUT

Fig 27A
(Plan)

DOWEL

FILLING PIECE

Fig 27C
(Plan)

DOTTED LINE DENOTES
ACTUAL CENTRE

Fig 27B

Fig 28A

Fig 28B

Fig 28C

Fig 28D

shown here you may find that a slanting edge cut into the face, and not into the thickness, is more suitable.

Damage is not necessarily confined to corners and can occur anywhere along the edge. Figs 28A and B show a way to cope with this by cutting away the damage; note particularly that the notch cut out of the edge is dovetail-shaped when viewed from above, and slightly wedge-shaped in the thickness. To fit this your repair piece must be, in effect, a dovetail-shaped wedge and it will help if you make it slightly oversize as shown. Fig 28A shows the damaged part ready for chopping out. Take great care to leave the edges clean and straight. Fig 28B shows the work after chopping out the damaged part ready to receive the repair block. In Fig 28C the block has been glued and replaced after shaping ready for the final rubbing down. Fig 28D shows the finished job.

◇ APPLIED BOLECTION MOULDINGS ◇

One of the most frequent problems with these types of mouldings is that a whole piece is missing, which emphasises the golden rule that if anything breaks off, replace it before it gets lost, otherwise the broken edges become so clogged with dirt, polish, etc, that a tightly fitting joint is impossible.

If just a comparatively small area is damaged, it can be dealt with in the same way as a stuck moulding. However, it does sometimes happen that a whole length of moulding becomes loose and you will then have to prise it off, using hot water sparingly to remove the old glue and keeping a wary eye open for any nails or pins which may have been used to refix it previously. Every part has to have dirt, old glue and any other detritus cleaned off, and an old chisel makes a good tool for this. When you glue the moulding back on you need to cramp it, particularly if it is a long piece which springs and will not lie flat; this is the occasion when upholstery-spring clamps (see page 24) come into their own, as you can link two or three together to span a width.

◇ WORKING MOULDINGS ◇

It seems to be appropriate at this point to explain how to shape the profile of a moulding.

The first essential is to make a template for the profile. If you have an odd piece of the moulding to be copied, this can be cut square across and pencilled around to transfer the shape to a piece of card or thin plywood. If not, you will have to use a 'moulding-transfer-former' (also called a 'template-former') as shown in Fig 29. This comprises a row of thin steel rods, usually 150 to 180 in number, which are held under slight tension in a metal frame so that when they are pressed against the moulding profile they will reproduce it, and you can pencil around the needle points to get the shaped outline either positive or in reverse.

If you have a spindle moulder, the actual machining of the profile is straightforward; similarly, if you have a set of moulding planes the job is easy enough, but for those who have neither we recommend the method shown in Figs 30A–F, which employs a combination of a saw-table and a scratch stock.

Proceeding stage by stage: Fig 30A shows the profile of a typical moulding. The initial step is to plane off a 'flat', and to do this the work must be held in a vice, which calls for two triangular packing pieces that can be pinned on. As the pin holes will be in the back faces of the moulding, which will eventually be hidden, they do not create a problem; the set-up is shown at Fig 30B.

Having removed the packing pieces once the planing is done, you need to make a cradle which serves both to hold the work while you are passing it over the saw and also to provide a square base for it to slide on (see Fig 30C). Use Scotch glue to fasten the work into the cradle as it is important that the moulding should be held firmly throughout its length; if one part springs then the saw-cuts will vary in depth. The glue can be removed once the work is done. Alternatively, the work can be held in place with a piece of glued brown paper, which can be taken out easily

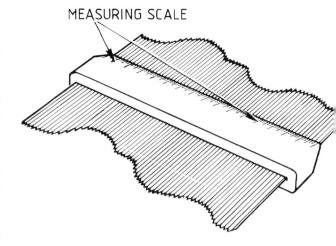

Fig 29

to separate the pieces when you have finished.

You can now make saw-cuts as shown at Fig 30D, turning the work to complete the cuts as in Fig 30E; you should then achieve the result illustrated in Fig 30F.

The next stage is to shape the shaded portions and the best way is to use a scratch stock – an old-fashioned device which is still useful in such circumstances. You can make one yourself, and Fig 31 shows you what it looks like. It consists of two pieces of wood which are mirror-images and which are screwed together with a blade between them; the blade is held tightly by the tension imparted by the screws. You will need to grind the blade to a reverse profile of the parts which have to be removed; the blade itself can be made from a piece of mild steel such as that used for cabinet scrapers, or from a piece of a broken bandsaw blade.

When glasspapering mouldings, never hold the glasspaper around your fingers to do the job or you will dub off the edges and lose that crispness of modelling which is so desirable. It doesn't take long to shape up a piece of scrap to the appropriate profile and wrap the glasspaper round it, and it does make a difference to the finished appearance.

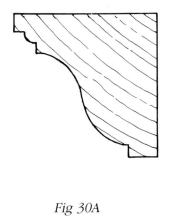

Fig 30A

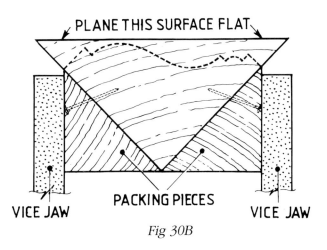

PLANE THIS SURFACE FLAT

PACKING PIECES

VICE JAW   VICE JAW

Fig 30B

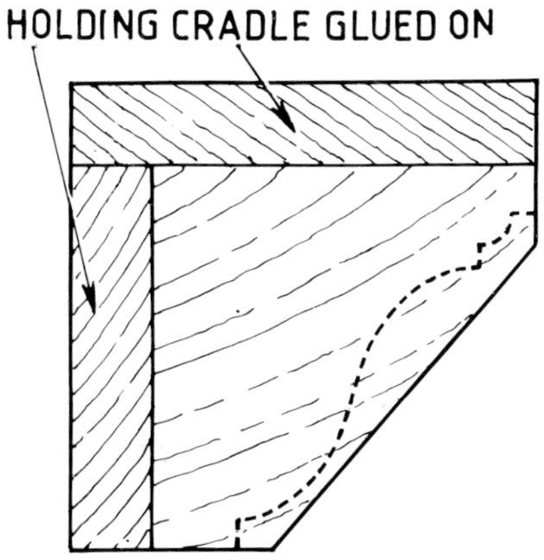

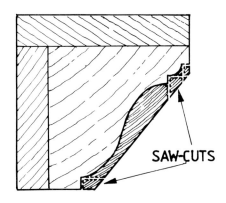

HOLDING CRADLE GLUED ON

Fig 30C

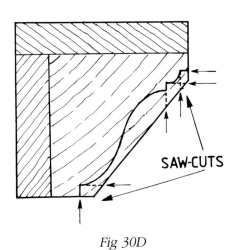

SAW-CUTS

Fig 30D

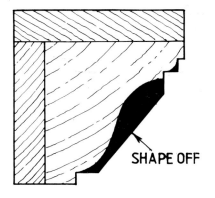

SAW-CUTS

Fig 30E

SHAPE OFF

Fig 30F

Fig 31

Fig 32A

Fig 32B

◇ CROSS-GRAINED MOULDINGS ◇

This kind of moulding was popular in the walnut era and comes in two types: the solid moulding (Fig 32), and the moulding which is rabbeted into the groundwork and then veneered over (Fig 33).

The sequence for repairing solid mouldings is shown in Fig 32A–D. In A the damaged section is shown marked ready for removal; B shows the gap. Great care is always necessary when working on cross-grained mouldings and it is usual to choose strong-grained timber. This, in turn, necessitates working along the grain, making splitting off a constant danger when using a chisel. In C the grain in the repair block is purposely running the wrong way so that the block shows in the photograph. The block has been fitted ready to be marked to the profile before working to shape. In D the block is shown glued into place after shaping, and is ready for a final rub-down prior to applying a finish.

Veneered mouldings of the type shown in Fig 33 can mean quite a problem if the moulding has broken away and taken some veneer with it. As a matter of routine, all traces of old glue, wax, polish etc have to be cleaned off and a new piece of moulding prepared. You then treat it as described in Fig 32 and, of course, you will have to repair the veneer as well with a patch which is as good a match as possible.

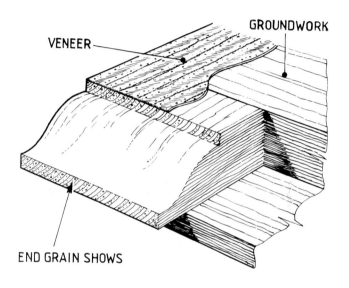

Fig 33

Fig 32C

Fig 32D

3 Veneering, Marquetry, Inlays and Bandings

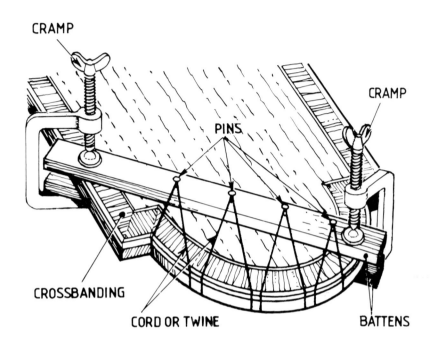

CRAMP

CRAMP

PINS

CROSSBANDING

CORD OR TWINE

BATTENS

Veneering as a craft dates back thousands of years to the Ancient Egyptians but was not introduced into England until the latter half of the seventeenth century, when it was brought over from the Continent by immigrant craftsmen. Veneering was never used as a cover-up for cheap timber and shoddy workmanship, except by an unscrupulous minority; rather, its purpose was to utilise the choicest and most beautifully figured woods as economically and effectively as possible. The timber used for veneer could not, in most cases, have been used in the solid; wood formations such as burrs, curls and fiddlebacks, for example, would be very difficult if not impossible to use in any other way.

Fig 34 shows how burrs, curls and fiddlebacks originate. Burrs are excrescences which grow on the tree, usually at the base, and are the result of buds which are arrested in the early stages of their growth by lack of nourishment; their appearance resembles a mass of tightly packed knots. The best known ones are from walnut trees, but there are others such as cherry, elm, oak and yew.

Curl figure originates from a crotch where either the main trunk divides or where a large branch joins it. Fiddleback figure is found mainly in mahoganies and sycamore and results from cutting through undulating layers of grain.

Until 1820, veneers were sawn by hand, and a laborious and arduous job it must have been; Fig 35 shows how it was done and is based on an illustration from a French book of 1774. Obviously this method could not yield very thin veneers of a uniform thickness. Such veneers are, on average, about 3–4mm thick, and these are the ones most likely to be found on old clock cases.

The first mention of a powered saw for cutting veneers in England was in 1805 (the source of the power, whether water-driven or by human or animal labour is not known); later in the same century steam-driven saws came into use but nevertheless veneers were still much thicker than modern ones, which are about 1mm thick; they are produced by adopting the principle of cutting the veneer mechanically with knives, either by the rotary, or the 'flat slicing', or the 'half-rotary' method (Fig 36). The rotary process is used for producing plain characterless veneers for plywood; flat slicing for long-grained figure; and the half-rotary for converting crotches and burrs.

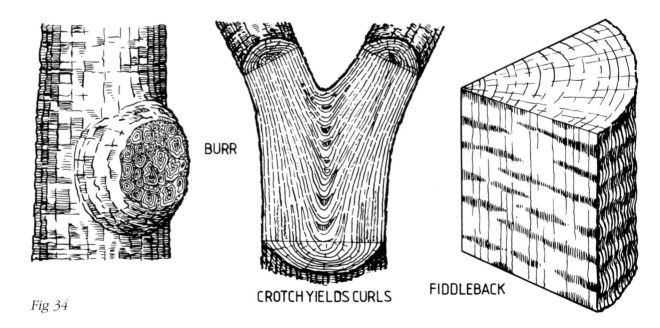

Fig 34   BURR   CROTCH YIELDS CURLS   FIDDLEBACK

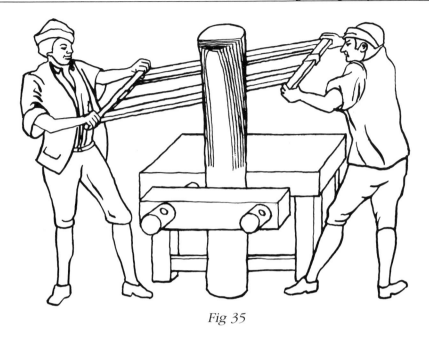

Fig 35

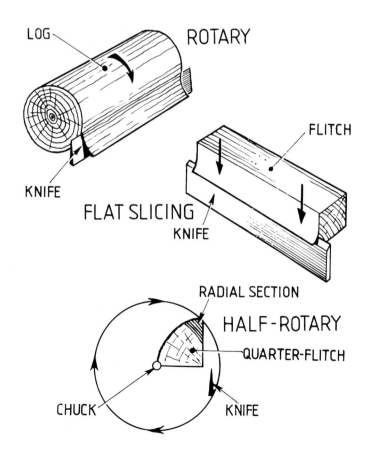

Fig 36

◇ REPAIRING DEFECTS IN VENEER ◇

The following are some points of guidance and methods to use for these repairs:

1 New glue will not adhere over old glue, nor will it stick properly to a dirty surface. It follows, then, that old glue and dirt must be cleared out, and a knife with a thin, pointed blade is best for this.

2 If you have to supply replacement veneer on an old clock case you will find that the original is the old saw-cut variety. Unless you are able to get the replacement from your own stock, or from a piece of old furniture, or from a furniture restorer, you will have to glue together two, or possibly three, pieces of modern veneer. If so, make sure that the grains of the pieces run at right angles to each other; always err on the side of more veneer rather than less as it helps if the replacement piece can be glasspapered level with the surrounding surface.

3 Veneers discolour with age, so even if the replacement piece is the same type and matches the grain, it will need staining (see page 63). Always do the staining and let it dry before gluing the piece in position – this is because the stain can make the veneer swell or warp and it is obviously best to have this under control before the final fixing is attempted.

4 If possible, always glue back a piece of veneer which has lifted, rather than cutting it out and replacing it. This may leave a gap around it but you can fill this with beaumontage (see page 59) tinted to the exact colour. If you have to glue back a piece of veneer which has become buckled as a result of being lifted, wipe off all the old glue from the back with a rag dampened in warm water or, in bad cases, scrape it off. Then dampen the veneer itself and cramp it between two flat blocks of wood to remove buckling; wait until it has thoroughly dried out and repeat the process if necessary.

5 The method of repairing chipped corners or edges depends largely on the pattern of the grain of the veneer. If it is wavy, as shown in Fig 37A, cut back into the sound veneer, using a sharp craft knife to follow the direction of the grain as much as possible; then ease the waste away.

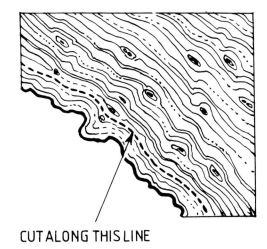

CUT ALONG THIS LINE

Fig 37A

Usually you can do this by inserting the tip of the knife blade under it and prising it up; if you heat the blade it will melt the glue. Sometimes, however, this method does not work and you then have to soften the glue by covering the defective patch with a damp rag and pressing down on to it with a warm soldering iron (for larger areas use a warm iron instead). This will melt the glue if it is Scotch glue, as it undoubtedly will be if the clock is over fifty years old. Be careful when doing this and if there is any sign of the colour turning red, stop immediately.

Next a pattern must be made for the replacement piece of veneer and you can do this by laying a thin piece of paper over the patch and rubbing across the edge with a pencil to produce an outline. Choose the replacement piece and match it for colour and grain. Paste the pattern to it and cut round it with a fine fretsaw, trimming it to the final shape with a file. Glue it down with the paper pattern still attached to prevent the veneer splitting, and rub it down with the pein of a hammer (Fig 37B), wiping off excess glue. Then stick some gummed paper tape over the joint to stop it opening as the glue dries out. Do not use a pressure sensitive tape, as when you come to peel it off it may bring tiny slivers of veneer with it; the paper tape will come off easily if you dampen it with water. Sometimes the new piece will persist in lifting and to cure it you will need

Fig 37B

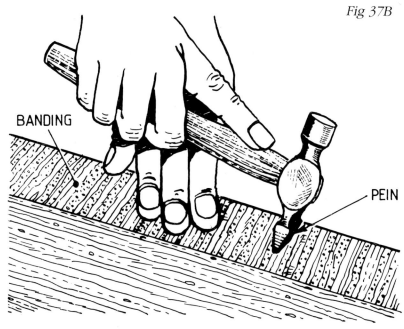

BANDING

PEIN

Fig 37C

CRAMP

VENEER

BLOCK

PAPER

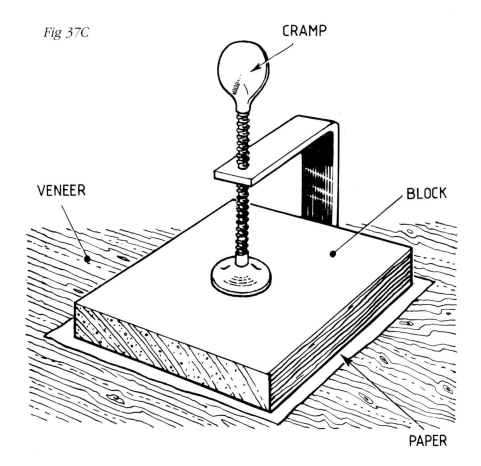

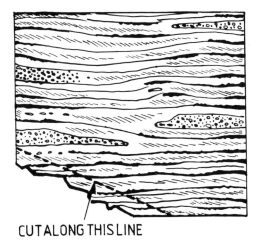

CUT ALONG THIS LINE

Fig 37D

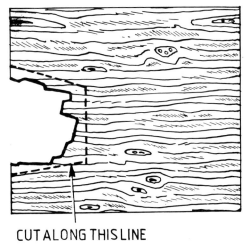

CUT ALONG THIS LINE

Fig 37E

to cramp a block of spare wood over it with a piece of waxed paper interposed (Fig 37C); if you are using Scotch glue, the block must be warmed so that it will not chill the glue and destroy its bonding properties, but this precaution is not necessary with any of the modern PVA or casein adhesives. When the veneer is straight-grained as in Figs 37D and 37E, the cutting outlines need to approximate to the shape of the repair, and the dotted lines show this.

6 There are two ways of treating splits in veneer according to whether or not there is underlying dirt. If the crack is clean, make a cross-shaped cut in the veneer as illustrated in Fig 38A, using the tip of a really sharp knife or an old razor blade so that you cut right through to the groundwork beneath. Then dampen the area slightly to render the veneer pliable, bend back the flaps gently and hold them open by wedging matchsticks under them (Fig 38B) so that they can dry out thoroughly. Next, work in fresh glue under them using an eye-dropper and a pointed piece of stick to push it under the flaps. Reposition the flaps, wipe away excess glue, cover the area with a piece of waxed paper and put a heavy weight on top; allow about twenty-four hours for the glue to set.

7 Blisters are caused in two ways, either because the area has become wet and the glue has softened and allowed the veneer (which has swelled) to rise; or because the glue has perished completely. What you do depends on whether or not the veneer has actually split.

If it has not, place a piece of soft cloth such as a duster over the area and gently put an electric iron on to it to soften the glue. The iron should be at its lowest heat; lift it every ten minutes or so and press the blister down to see if the glue holds. When it does, use the same treatment as for cracked veneers, namely a warm block of wood and a heavy weight.

If the veneer has split, there is no point in introducing fresh glue until the perished glue (and any dirt) has been removed. This means that you will have to cut out the raised pieces to leave an open patch: clean the pieces and the patch thoroughly and glue the pieces back. Cramp up as already described.

8 Replacing missing pieces in a length of straight crossbanding can be dealt with in the same way as replacing patches of veneer. But the matter gets complicated when you are dealing with the type of curved crossbanding found on a hood or trunk door because of working the veneer round the curve and holding any associated strings or lines in position while the glue dries out.

Fig 39A shows how the replacement pieces of crossbanding are arranged radially round the curve, rather like a series of keystones. The pieces protrude beyond the edge and, once the glue has set, the surplus can be trimmed off with a sharp chisel.

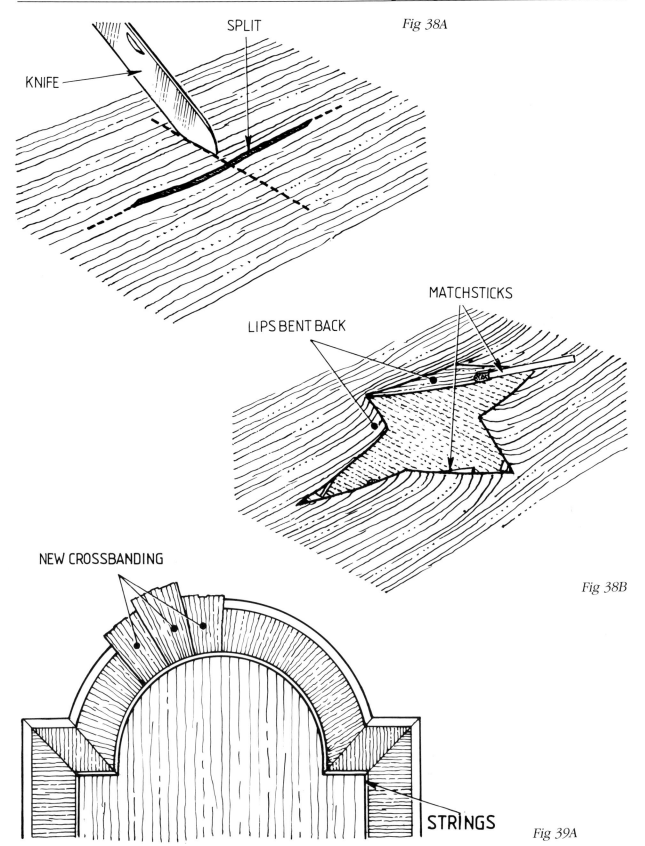

Fig 38A

KNIFE

SPLIT

MATCHSTICKS

LIPS BENT BACK

Fig 38B

NEW CROSSBANDING

STRINGS

Fig 39A

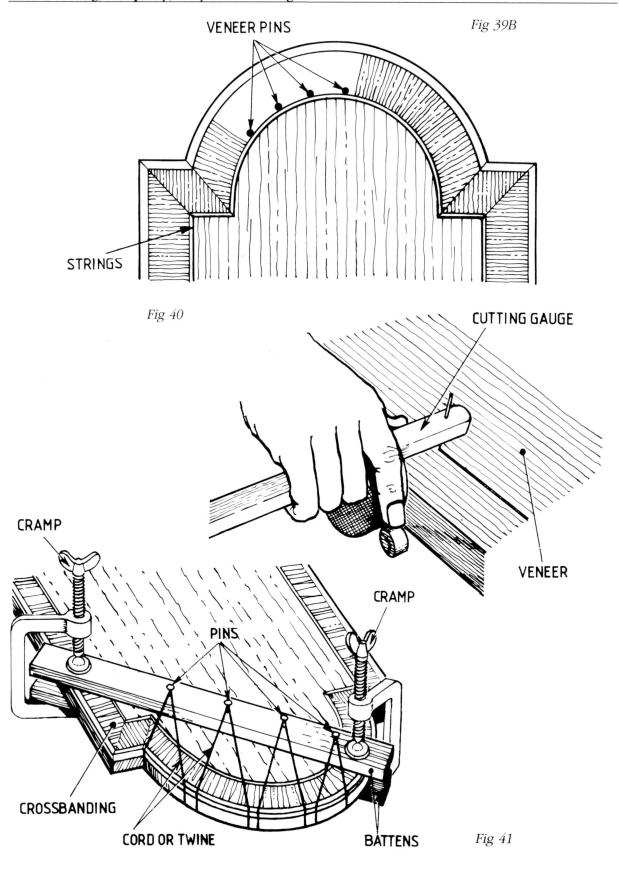

VENEER PINS

Fig 39B

STRINGS

Fig 40

CUTTING GAUGE

VENEER

CRAMP

CRAMP

PINS

CROSSBANDING

CORD OR TWINE

BATTENS

Fig 41

If there is a line inlaid around the inner edge of the crossbanding and some of it is missing you will almost certainly have to make some yourself. Until comparatively recently lines were sold in bundles and ranged in thickness from 'hair' lines which were less than 1mm square up to 3mm (⅛in) square, but you may find it difficult to locate a source. 'Strings' are very similar, except that they are larger and not necessarily square; the method of making both is explained in Chapter 9.

To hold the line in place you need to drive in part way a few veneer pins as shown in Fig 39B. But first a groove must be cut for it in the new crossbanding you have just laid. Do this by running a cutting gauge round the edge (Fig 40); if you do not have such a gauge, make yourself a 'scratch stock' (as described on page 32) with a suitable cutter which will do the job just as well.

You can use the scratch stock to cut the rabbet for the stringing which often borders the crossbanding on the outside. Such stringing will need a little steaming to persuade it to bend; holding it in the steam from a kettle should suffice (wear gloves to avoid scalded hands). The next problem is to hold it in position while the glue sets and this is resolved by cramping two lengths of scrap

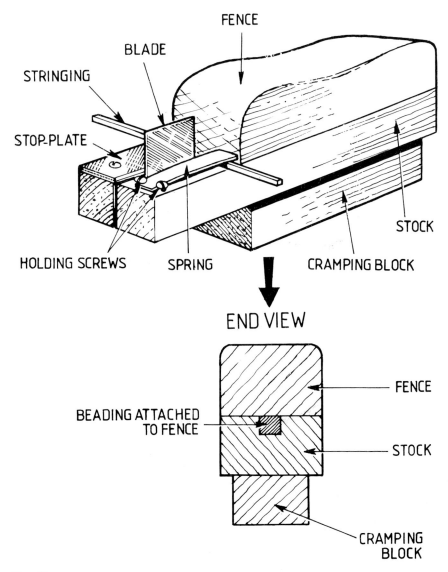

Fig 42

timber together, one on each side of the work; each length has a few nails partly driven in and some strong tape or string is laced around them as shown in Fig 41. This will effectively keep the stringing in place while the glue sets.

Lines and strings need trimming to the correct thickness and this can be done with a sizing gauge (Fig 42). It is a tool you can make yourself. It has a stock which consists of two identical pieces screwed together with the cutter fixed between them. The cutter is best made from a piece of scraper steel, which can be bought quite easily from any good ironmonger, and its edge should be bevelled at an angle of about 30 degrees on a grindstone and then finished on an oilstone. Underneath the stock and screwed to it is a block which can be cramped in the vice; on the top surface at the working end is a steel stop-plate which prevents the movable fence from being pushed forward too far. The fence has a 10×10mm (⅜×⅜in) bead screwed and glued centrally along its underside and this runs in a corresponding channel worked in the top faces of the stock. The length of this channel must be arranged to end at the stop-plate so that the fence can be slid right up to the edge of the cutter. The last component is a piece of spring steel held down by a couple of screws, and this serves to hold the stringing firmly while it is being trimmed. To use the gauge, lay one end of the stringing in place as shown; push the fence against it with one hand and pull it through with the other.

◇ REPAIRS TO MARQUETRY ◇

These kinds of repairs are a headache and unless you have a good stock of pieces of different veneers, and unlimited patience, it is almost always best to leave such jobs to a professional restorer.

However, assuming that you want to make the attempt, we will deal first with small pieces that are missing. To get the required shape for the replacement piece, lay a piece of thin white paper over the gap and rub it with a soft pencil to obtain the outline. Paste the paper on to the replacement veneer with Scotch glue, as it will help to stop the veneer cracking, and then cut around the outline before sticking it down into the gap, which must have been thoroughly cleaned out. Wipe off excess glue and then put a piece of waxed paper over the work, finally putting a heavy weight on top. Do not attempt to remove the pasted-on paper until the glue has set completely, when it can be removed.

It is quite likely that you may be confronted with a piece of marquetry where one or two comparatively large patches have lifted. It is often recommended that you put some glue on a thin-bladed knife, such as a palette knife, and introduce it under the loose stuff and then put a weight on the work to hold the veneer down until the glue sets. Try this by all means, as it sometimes works. Usually, however, the remains of old glue and dust prevent the fresh glue from adhering.

An alternative method is to insert the tip of a knife blade or a thin chisel and prise the loose veneer away as far as it will go without cracking; then gently clean out the space with a cotton bud dampened with hot water, introduce fresh glue, and place a heavy weight on top. Some authorities advise softening the veneer on its surface to make it more pliable, using a damp rag. Unfortunately, this is effective only if the polish is removed first as, naturally, water will not penetrate it; alternatively, tiny holes can be pricked right through the veneer. Both methods bring problems in their wake, either of repolishing to match, or of disguising the presence of the holes.

Making new marquetry is a fascinating craft and offers unlimited scope for self-expression. It is far too large a subject to deal with here, and we suggest you study W. A. Lincoln's excellent book *The Art and Practice of Marquetry* published by Thames and Hudson. We do, however, deal with making oysters and marquetry fans in Chapter 9.

◇ MOTHER-OF-PEARL AND IVORY ◇

Both these materials were widely employed in decorative work on clock cases, usually in conjunction with boulle work, and although supplies are now very scarce you may find some in the dark corners of a warehouse somewhere.

There are several qualities of mother-of-pearl, the rarest being the blue, green and pink colours; there is the Japanese kind, which is wavy in pattern and varies in colour; and finally the ordinary 'snail' type. The material is usually about 1.5mm (¹⁄₁₆in) thick and is supplied in irregular-shaped pieces from 25–50mm (1–2in) wide.

Although it can be cut with a very fine-toothed saw and filed to shape, it is advisable to reinforce it by backing it with a stiff veneer with paper sandwiched between. Scotch glue should be used so that the backing paper and veneer can be removed easily by dampening with warm water.

To ensure a good bond, roughen the back of the mother-of-pearl with a file and prick the groundwork; it is a good idea to mix a little plaster of Paris with the Scotch glue so that the mixture will fill up the irregularities on the back of the pearl which might otherwise cause cracking if pressure (such as cramps) is applied. In fact, it would probably be better to use a comparatively light weight, such as a plane, to apply pressure, rather than cramps. The glue should be used quite hot.

The face of mother-of-pearl is so smooth as to need little polishing but where needed you can use a fine file, followed by the finest grade of abrasive paper, and finally pumice powder and rottenstone. If the pearl is inlaid into bare wood, take care that the very fine powder does not get into the grain of the surrounding wood, which should be sealed first with a coat of clear shellac that can be removed easily after the job is done.

Ivory can be sawn and filed in the same way as mother-of-pearl, and is laid on to the groundwork in a similar manner. Polishing is also the same except that the final stage is to buff it with a soft rag and whiting.

4 Repairs to Ormolu, Boulle and Lacquer Work

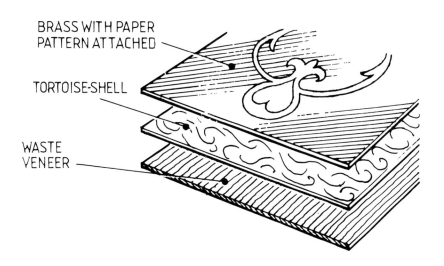

BRASS WITH PAPER
PATTERN ATTACHED

TORTOISE-SHELL

WASTE
VENEER

Before discussing the methods of remedying defects in ormolu, boulle and lacquer work, we will set these crafts in their historical backgrounds, as a knowledge of how they originated and developed will help you to understand the techniques involved. However, if you are thinking of using either ormolu or boulle to decorate a new clock case, then you are in for a difficult time as ormolu involves casting in bronze, and boulle work needs tortoise-shell, which cannot legally be offered for sale. Certainly, you should be able to tackle découpage, which is a form of lacquering, and we will be discussing various ways to do the work.

◇ ORMOLU ◇

The word 'ormolu' derives from the French *bronze dorée d'or moulu* ('gilt bronze') and in the eighteenth century in France some of the most magnificent examples came from the *fondeurs*, who cast and chased various metals, and the *doreurs*, who were the gilders. Ormolu was used for a multitude of purposes such as candelabra, door furniture, decorating fireplaces, mounts for furniture and mounts for clock cases. It served three purposes: decoration; as protection for vulnerable points; and to help reinforce joints and to make the framework rigid.

The first step in making an ormolu mount was to produce a model in wax or wood and this was then cast in bronze; next, it was tooled and chased to a perfect finish by a *ciseleur*, and then gilded. Often, the bronze was merely dipped in acid and then lacquered, but for a superior finish, it was gilded by the 'fire-gilding' (or 'mercury') process.

This involved making a spongy paste of gold dust and mercury and applying it to the work with a brush, making sure that any crevices were coated. Enough mercury was mixed in to allow it to bite into the surface of the metal, taking the gold dust with it; the longer it was left to do so, the thicker and more effective the gilding, although there was a time limit after which the metal itself began to crumble away. At the end of this stage the work was washed in water and any mercury or gold dust was recovered for future use. Next, the work was heated in a small forge and then allowed to cool before being washed again, first in a weak acid and then in water, after which it was dried in heated sawdust. It was then ready for burnishing and subsequent lacquering. The whole process was expensive, and the fumes of the mercury were very injurious to the health of the workers. Today the bronze is coated with gold by an electrical process.

Cleaning ormolu

Never be tempted to use metal polish to clean ormolu; it is the injudicious use of this kind of polish which has removed the gold from many an antique mount, leaving the bronze exposed and certain, eventually, to tarnish. You must, of course, remove any mounts before cleaning and they are often pinned into place.

Proprietary cleaners are obtainable but there is an easy one that you can make up for yourself by shredding a cake of good quality toilet soap into a jug of warm water, adding about half a cupful of liquid ammonia, and stirring well. Apply this to the ormolu, using an old toothbrush *gently* to get into the crevices, then rinse off.

Various repairs

Small spots and patches can be touched in quite easily with gold lacquer, and this can also be used to gild the whole mount provided you take care not to produce streaks. Try to use the older-type spirit lacquer as it does not dry so rapidly as modern synthetic lacquers, and any mistakes can be removed easily with a solvent such as turpentine substitute (white spirit). You can also use wax gilt, or a gold powder/quick-drying size mixture, both of which are described in Chapter 6. Finally, you could have the mount re-gilded professionally. This usually results in a new-looking, bright finish which, although suitable for a new clock case, would look out of place on an old one.

◇ BOULLE MARQUETRY ◇

This is a form of marquetry using thin sheets of brass and tortoiseshell, and it was developed and perfected by André Charles Boulle (1642–1732). It is sometimes referred to as 'Buhl', but this word is usually reserved for the products made at the beginning of the nineteenth century, when the craft enjoyed a revival after having fallen into disuse during the eighteenth century. Essentially, the process consisted of holding a sheet of brass and a sheet of tortoiseshell together while they were sawn around a pattern stuck to the upper sheet; when separated the sheets were interchangeable and if the brass sheet predominated and was laid into a tortoiseshell ground, the design was called *première-partie* (or inlay of the first part), while the reverse – tortoiseshell predominating over the brass – was called *contre-partie* (or counter-inlay). Frequently other materials such as mother-of-pearl or silver were also incorporated into the pattern, and the metal was often elaborately engraved.

But this is merely an outline, and before going on to explain the procedure in greater detail, we will consider the best ways to deal with any defects in existing boulle work.

Repairs to boulle work

The most common faults are the result of poor adhesion: this was a problem that bedevilled the old-time craftsmen and, if it is any comfort, one complete wall at the French palace of Fontainebleau which was covered with boulle work suffered badly from delamination and had to be replaced!

If you are confronted with pieces of brass sheet which have lifted, or which are loose, the repair work is not too difficult. The glue used in the old days was based on Scotch glue with the addition of garlic; it can be dissolved easily by applying warm water very carefully and sparingly – a cotton-wool bud makes a good applicator. When all the old glue has been cleaned out, let the area dry out thoroughly without artificial heating; if you can get at it, roughen the underside of the brass with a small file to form a key for the adhesive. Any epoxy resins which are suitable for

bonding metal to wood will do the work perfectly. But if you are restoring a piece you must use a reversible glue such as the Salisbury glue mentioned below.

Working with tortoiseshell

Dealing with loose tortoiseshell is rather tricky, and replacing a missing piece even trickier. Remove old glue in the same way as for brass and allow the area to dry thoroughly without artificial heat. There are two problems which may now present themselves. The first is that the tortoiseshell was often glued down to a piece of coloured paper, the purpose being to let the colour glow through the translucent shell. If the paper is spoiled or missing it will have to be replaced. Sometimes the underside of the shell was painted to give a similar result, and in this event may need to be touched up with artist's oil colours. You need a transparent water-clear adhesive if you are gluing the tortoiseshell over coloured paper; in the old days, Salisbury glue was used (this was made from animal skins instead of the bones, hooves, etc employed in making Scotch glue) and this sometimes had flake-white or plaster of Paris added to it to change its brown colour to a creamy hue.

The favourite tortoiseshell was that of the hawksbill tortoise as it had black, yellow and flame markings. It was difficult to lay successfully as it was brittle and therefore it had to be coaxed around a surface; this was achieved by steaming to soften it and using a caul (such as a sandbag) to hold it in place while the glue set. For very sharp bends a piece of linen was glued temporarily to the face to prevent it cracking, and was removed by damping with warm water to soften the glue. The back of the shell needed to be roughened to form a key for the glue, and this had to be done very carefully as heavy marks could show through; you will find that a light papering with medium glasspaper should suffice.

If you are lucky enough to have some pieces of tortoiseshell you must look after them to keep them supple. Do this by making a paste with senna powder and olive oil and applying this to the shell with the palm of your hand once a week. Genuine tortoiseshell is unobtainable these days as tortoises are protected in the interests of conservation.

Preparing the brass

Before proceeding to describe the cutting and assembly of boulle work, a few notes on the type of brass used and its preparation may be helpful.

There is a special kind of brass called 'gilding metal' which is made for use in decorative work; it contains a higher proportion of copper and zinc than ordinary hard brass. Check that the colour is not too red – which can happen if there is too much copper – because the brass should be as bright and as yellow as possible in order to attain the best contrast. If the colour passes the test, then the brass can be used without further treatment.

There are, however, other kinds of brass sheet which are more readily available and a simple test will show how hard they are. Bend up one corner of the sheet: if it bends easily and stays bent, then the brass is soft; if you can only bend it with difficulty then the brass is medium hard; hard brass cannot be bent at all, or only with the greatest effort. It can be annealed to make it more malleable by coating one surface with a thin film of ordinary household soap and holding it over a gas ring until the heat turns the soap film brown and makes it bubble: don't quench it as it may crack; leave it to cool off in its own time.

The back of the brass sheet (that is, the side which will be glued down) needs to be roughened with a rasp to provide a key for the glue. But before you do this, rub the surface with a piece of garlic, or wipe it over with a cloth dampened with vinegar: both will act as weak mordants.

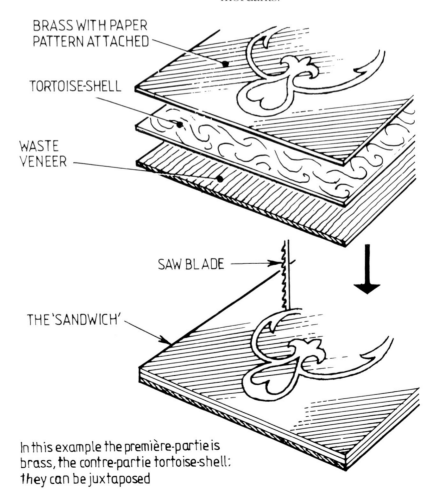

BRASS WITH PAPER PATTERN ATTACHED

TORTOISE-SHELL

WASTE VENEER

SAW BLADE

THE 'SANDWICH'

In this example the première-partie is brass, the contre-partie tortoise-shell: they can be juxtaposed

Fig 43

Cutting the inlays

As already mentioned, there are two components in boulle work; the first (*première-partie*) consists of brass inlaid into a tortoiseshell background, and the second (*contre-partie*) is its reverse, namely tortoiseshell inlaid into a brass background. This involves making up a 'sandwich' consisting of the brass sheet with the paper pattern to be cut out pasted to it, followed by the tortoiseshell, and then a sheet of veneer at the bottom which will take the swarf from the saw teeth – the sandwich is illustrated in Fig 43.

The big problem is how to hold the sandwich together while it is being sawn. You can glue the pieces to one another with Scotch glue which can be removed with warm water after sawing; or you can hold them with small thumbscrews. If you do use the cramping method, it is a good idea to interpose a sheet of waxed paper somewhere in the sandwich, as it will lubricate the saw. Although the old-time craftsmen used saws made from clock springs, you can make life a lot easier

with a modern metal-sawing blade, or one of the universal types which cut metal, wood, plastic, etc. Add to this one of the small powered fretsaws as used by model makers, and you have the perfect set-up.

If you saw with the blade held vertically, you will find that when the two parties are assembled there is a small gap (equal to the thickness of the blade) all round the pattern. This problem confronted Boulle himself and he solved it by making a virtue of necessity and filling the gap with a black composition paste which accentuated the contrast between the two materials; you can do the same, using wood-filler tinted black.

There is another way, however, which will eliminate the gap, and this is to cut at a slight angle so that the pieces have bevelled edges which will slide into each other and give a snug fit. If you are using a powered fretsaw all you need do is to tilt the table; the angle of the tilt needs to be just enough to compensate for the thickness of the saw blade, as illustrated in Fig 44.

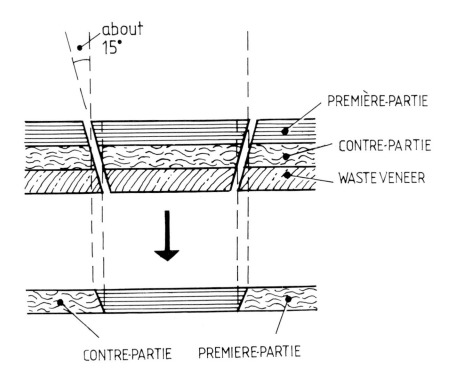

In this example the première-partie is brass, the contre-partie tortoise-shell; they can be juxtaposed

Fig 44

◇ LACQUERING ◇

True Oriental lacquer was known to the Chinese as long ago as 2000BC, but by the fifteenth century Japanese craftsmen who had been taught by the Chinese were turning out better work than their tutors; and, in fact, lacquered goods imported by the various European trading companies in the seventeenth and eighteenth centuries were predominantly Japanese, and not Chinese. The various names given to these goods, such as Canton-ware, Bantam-ware and Coromandel-ware did not refer to their origin but to the port of shipment.

Lacquer is entirely different from shellac: the latter refers to the incrustations of sap from various trees formed by the feeding habits of an insect called *Coccus lacca*; the incrustations are processed to become what we call shellac, and what was known in the seventeenth and eighteenth centuries as 'seed lac'. The word 'lac' derives from the Hindi *lakh* and the Sanskrit *laksa*; both mean 100,000 and this describes the enormous number of insects required to produce it. Real lacquer as used by the Chinese and Japanese comes from the sap of the lac tree (also called the Japanese lacquer tree and the varnish tree, and botanically, *Rhus vernicifera*). The bark is slit horizontally and the black, tar-like sap oozes out and is collected – the process being rather like tapping rubber trees for latex.

As a matter of interest the tree, which is one of the sumac family, is grown in Britain but is usually restricted to arboreta or private collections of unusual trees. This is just as well as the sap is highly toxic and causes a very irritating rash: we have heard of an ancient Chinese lacquered vase which had been buried for centuries, on which the lacquer was still toxic.

In addition to the highest grade lacquer made from the sap, another one of inferior quality was made from boiling twigs and small branches. The raw material was processed by manufacturers who had their own secret formulae and this was the stumbling block – they steadfastly refused to divulge the information! Although some European countries tried to discover it by bringing over Oriental craftsmen, they were unlucky as the craftsmen consistently used inferior lacquers, and the secret has not been disclosed to this day.

Japanning

This is the European version of Oriental lacquer, and was once all the rage in England, France and Italy. At its worst it consisted of coats of paint covered with a coat of clear French polish; at its best it involved the use of coloured enamels with designs of gold and silver laid on them. In the seventeenth century the art was so popular that in 1688 John Stalker and George Parker published their *Treatise of Japanning, Varnishing and Gilding*, which purported to be a 'Compleat Discovery of those Arts', and this was the book which encouraged many a lady to try her hand at japanning any piece of furniture or bric-a-brac which took her fancy!

Repairs to lacquer work

As may be gathered from the foregoing, both lacquering and japanning are skilful techniques and we would advise against attempting to repair any kind of damage or defects; about the most we would suggest is that any tiny spots where the colour has chipped away could be touched in. Any more than this and you could easily do more harm than good, so leave it to the professional restorer.

◇ DÉCOUPAGE ◇

This decorative technique was invented and practised in Italy during the seventeenth century, where it was called *l'arte povero* ('the poor man's art'), and it spread first to France (*l'art scriban*) and then to the rest of Europe, including Britain.

It consists, in principle, of gluing coloured prints to wooden surfaces and then covering them with many coats of varnish so that they resemble hand-painted Chinese and Japanese lacquer ware. (The process can also be used to decorate glass and porcelain, and it was enormously popular in the late seventeenth and early eighteenth centuries as an artistic hobby for fashionable ladies, who called it 'japanning'.)

The same technique can be employed on clock cases, as many were adorned with découpage in the old days, particularly on the waists of drop-dial wall clocks. We can even improve on the results, as old work was covered with a shellac-based varnish which inevitably darkened over the years but today we can utilise glues and varnishes which should retain their clarity for a long time. However, these should not be used for restoring jobs.

The first step is to glasspaper the wood to a satin smoothness with progressively finer grades of glasspaper; some tiny fibres in the wood may refuse to be removed – get rid of them by 'raising the grain', that is damping the wood with clean cold water so that the fibres absorb it and stand upright. As soon as the water has dried you will be able to glasspaper them off easily.

The kind of print you choose depends on your own taste, of course, and you can use a putty-type adhesive (such as Blu-Tack) to hold it in position temporarily while you study the effect. Next, the wood must be sealed before the print is glued down so that the colours will not bleed. The method depends on whether or not you want an antique appearance. If you do, use clear shellac (or white French polish); if not, spray on two or three coats of acrylic sealer which can be obtained in aerosol cans from art shops.

For antique and restoration work use gum arabic to glue on the print; this is the normal adhesive for sticking paper and is sold by stationers. For other work the normal white PVA woodworking adhesive is suitable. In both cases, the print should be rolled down after gluing with a rubber roller (as used by photographers) to expel all air bubbles, and then left to dry.

The varnish for antique pieces needs to be clear spirit varnish, and the print must be given an initial coat of glue size. This varnishing is a long job as you should put on about twenty coats, allowing each one to dry for twenty-four hours and then glasspapering it lightly with the finest grade of glasspaper, the last coat being left unpapered. Put the varnish on to the surrounding wood as well, as the idea is that it should be impossible to feel the edges of the print under the build-up of varnish.

For a modern job use a polyurethane lacquer, applying the same number of coats. This kind of lacquer sets quickly and can be touch-dry in an hour or so at the most, but do not be deceived into thinking that you can then apply the next coat. The fact is that solvents will continue to evaporate for up to six hours, and to be safe it is best to leave an interval of eight hours. You will not need to glasspaper the separate coats until the tenth one when you can do so with wet-and-dry paper (finest grade), used wet; then do the same with every third coat until the last, which is left alone.

Your biggest enemy is dust, both airborne and that left from glasspapering. Protect the work from the first by erecting some kind of a covering for it, and from the second by wiping away the dust with a 'tack rag', which you can make by sprinkling a few drops of varnish on a lint-free cloth and rubbing it in until the cloth is tacky.

5 Dealing with Finishes

Before you even contemplate doing anything about a piece which appears to need repolishing, it is as well to find out everything you can about the finishes that were used in the old days, and learn how to identify them.

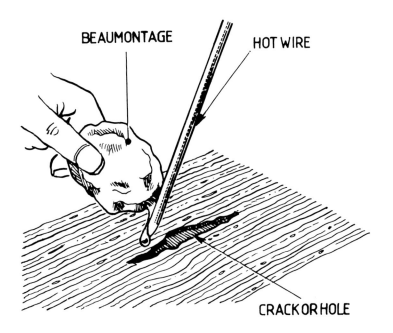

BEAUMONTAGE

HOT WIRE

CRACK OR HOLE

◇ VARNISHES ◇

Despite the disparaging remarks made about it by some connoisseurs of antiques, varnish was the most-used finish up to the 19th century. It was almost always subsequently followed by regular waxing over the years which mellowed the glittery appearance of the new varnish and formed the basis of the satin-like patina that only careful attention can give. In many cases the constant application of the wax rubbed away most of the varnish, except that which penetrated the pores of the grain where it formed an effective barrier to keep out dust and grime.

Sheraton does not mention varnish in his *Cabinet Dictionary* (*c*1790), but recommends applying fine brickdust with linseed oil, rubbed down with a cork block; presumably this would fill the grain and colour the wood. During the eighteenth century, and certainly over the period when mahogany was popular, varnish was used, but was preceded by a coat of linseed oil; often, bruised alkanet roots (*Anchusa tinctoria*; a variety of our garden plant from the Mediterranean) were steeped in the oil to give it a warm red colour. The resulting hue was a matter of trial and error, which probably accounts for the differing shades of mahogany found on many pieces of old furniture.

As an interesting alternative to the use of brickdust, Stalker and Parker recommended using Dutch rushes for the final rubbing-down of the raw timber before polishing; and in the Middle Ages rough fish skin or shark skin was used – which makes one appreciate modern abrasive papers! Stalker and Parker's *Treatise of Japanning, Varnishing and Gilding* has been regarded for many years as an indispensable handbook.

Some readers may wish to reproduce the old type of varnish, so the various kinds and their uses are described below; the practical application of all varnishes is explained later in the chapter.

Technically, a varnish is a solution of selected resins in a solvent; the resins can be gum opal, gum damar, sandarac, or shellac; the solvents include methylated spirits (alcohol), pure turpentine or turpentine substitute (white spirit), raw linseed oil, cotton-seed oil, or wood naphtha. The types of resin and oil used determine such characteristics of the varnish as the drying time, surface hardness, and the elasticity of the coating.

There are two principal traditional varnishes. The spirit varnishes – hard spirit varnish and 'flatting varnish' (which dries matt) – consist of shellac, sandarac, or any other brittle gum dissolved in alcohol or pure turpentine. Oil varnish, which includes white, pale, medium and dark grades, has the resins dissolved in an oil (usually linseed) with a small amount of pure turpentine added to increase workability. It is important to bear in mind that spirit varnishes dry by evaporation of the solvent into the air, while oil varnishes are slower to dry as the oil absorbs oxygen from the air and solidifies with the gum to form a preservative skin.

French polish

Another (not so old) finish is French polish, which is a type of varnish; it arrived in England from France in about 1820.

◇ FINISHING METHODS ◇

As this was just when the longcase clock was going out of fashion, you are not likely to meet any such clocks that have French polish as the original finish. We use the word 'original' because the Victorians did strip many clocks and repolish them, often with French polish, and these are the ones you might have to deal with. If you should meet with this finish do not attempt to restore it yourself as it is definitely a job for a professional. The basic ingredients are shellac (see Lacquering, page 65) dissolved in methylated spirits, and the kind of shellac governs the type of polish; the best-known kinds are white,

transparent white, orange, button and garnet. White polish is creamy in colour and tends to tint light-coloured work slightly grey; transparent white has about the same colouring tendency as water; orange polish imparts a warm red tint; button polish is yellowish-orange in colour and gives a golden hue on light-coloured work but should not be used on warm, dark stains as it tends to kill the colour – garnet is the one to use on such stains. All of these can be bought from polish suppliers although you can make them up yourself. See page 68.

◇ STRIPPING OLD FINISHES AND ◇ USING STOPPINGS

If you browse through books on repolishing old furniture you will come across many recipes for home-made strippers, some of which read like a witches' brew for skinning people alive! Our advice is to disregard them all and use a good proprietary stripper made by a reputable manufacturer. Follow the instructions exactly and remember that, where possible, the stripper should be applied to a horizontal surface rather than a vertical one for the best results. Many strippers are destructive of synthetic materials – so protect your clothes and don't wear a nylon shirt. Wear industrial-type gloves, and if any splashes get on your skin, wash them off immediately with plenty of water.

Use cheap bristle brushes (not synthetic) which can be discarded, as the stripper will probably spoil them. Other useful equipment includes plenty of cotton rags, and several empty tins into which you can pour off the stripper in handy quantities – save a couple of tins to keep the brushes in and to catch the sludge. Instead of standing the work on old newspapers, use opened-out and flattened cardboard cartons from the supermarket, as they do not flap about or become saturated so quickly.

Remove as much brassware as possible before

starting and mask off any glass with proper masking tape, not pressure sensitive tapes; it is best to remove the glass entirely, if this can be done. Apply the stripper gently in short strokes, avoiding 'runs' as far as possible. When the stripper has done its work, push off the sludge with a piece of wood with one side shaved to a sharp edge. This will never dig in or scratch the surface as a metal knife will. On obstinate spots, rub gently with a piece of fine steel wool dipped in the stripper; clean out the nooks and crannies of carved areas with a small bristle brush and an assortment of small wooden sticks.

There may well be a few cracks, holes and stains to be dealt with before the work can be refinished. If the work is to be waxed (but not varnished or French polished) you can make up your own stopping for cracks or holes; it is called 'beaumontage' and its great advantage is that you can add exactly the right amount of powder colour to match the surrounding wood. To make it, mix equal quantities of beeswax (yellow for light-coloured woods, brown for dark-coloured) with crushed resin, add a few flakes of shellac, and melt it all in a tin immersed in hot water, but not over a naked flame as it is inflammable. This stopping will be suitable for light-coloured

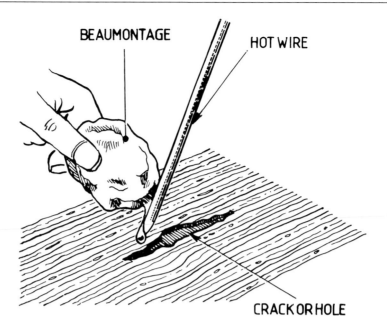

Fig 45

BEAUMONTAGE

HOT WIRE

CRACK OR HOLE

woods as it is, but you can add powder colour for darker woods, bearing in mind that it must match the stained colour of the wood if you are, in fact, staining it. To use it, hold a piece of hot metal (such as a length of wire) over the hole and press a piece of the beaumontage against it; the stopping will melt and run into the hole (Fig 45). For varnishes and French polish use one of the proprietary stopping mixtures, which are made in a variety of shades to match differently coloured surfaces.

You can often disguise small scratches by rubbing along them diagonally with the pulp of a walnut, a Brazil nut, or a pecan, which will gradually darken the scratch to match its surroundings. On woods which have been finished with oil, rub the scratch with the finest grade of steel wool dipped in a light machine oil or boiled linseed oil. Rub with the grain and finish by giving the whole surface a wipe over with a lint-free cloth (cheese-cloth or cotton which will not leave fluff) which has been moistened with boiled linseed oil, and then rub off with a dry cloth.

If the finish is French polish, damp a cloth with methylated spirits and gently soften the edges of the scratch and move the polish to fill the cracks; the same procedure can be employed with a varnished finish, except that pure turpentine (or turpentine substitute) should replace the methylated spirits.

◇ IDENTIFYING THE FINISH ◇

The treatment for scratches mentioned above gives you a valuable clue for identifying an old or faded finish. Apply the solvents to a small, inconspicuous part of the job and check to see if the finish comes off on the cloth. Methylated spirits will dissolve French polish but not varnish; turpentine (or turpentine substitute) will dissolve varnishes but not French polish. If you have to deal with a clock case which has been cellulose-finished, only cellulose thinners will have any effect.

◇ CLEANERS AND REVIVERS ◇

A good method for cleaning light soiling is to wipe the work with a soft, lint-free cloth dipped in warm water to which pure soap flakes have been added – you can pare them from a cake of toilet soap with a potato peeler. Do not wet the surface too much, particularly if it is veneered, otherwise you may damage it; so deal with a small area at a time and wipe it dry before going on to the next. An efficient cleaner for bad soiling is a mixture consisting of 1.2 litres (1 quart) of hot water and 3 tablespoons of boiled linseed oil. Keep it hot in a separate container of boiling water and not on a naked flame, as it is inflammable. Rub the affected areas with a soft cloth dipped in the solution, and then wipe dry with another cloth, which will bring out the effectiveness of the oil as a polish.

Sometimes a surface will have a cloudy, hazy appearance and in such cases a 'reviver' will work wonders. Proprietary brands are obtainable, and it is important to follow the manufacturers' instructions exactly; however, the following are some recipes for simple ones you can make up for yourself:

1 Suitable for all surfaces: 4 parts raw linseed oil; 1 part terebene (to speed up drying time); 12 parts vinegar. Apply with a soft lint-free cloth.

2 Suitable for all surfaces: 1 part raw linseed oil; 1 part vinegar. Apply as above.

3 Suitable for French polished surfaces only: 1 part clear French polish (shellac); 2 parts liquid paraffin. Apply as above, but fine-graded steel wool can be used in stubborn cases.

4 Suitable for varnished finishes only: 1 part raw linseed oil; 1 part pure turpentine. Apply as above.

5 Boil 600ml (1pt) of distilled water, shred about 100g (4oz) of any good quality soap into it and let it dissolve completely. In a separate receptacle have ready 600ml (1pt) of pure turpentine or turpentine substitute (white spirit) and add to it 50g (2oz) of best bleached beeswax and 50g (2oz) of white paraffin wax. Heat to dissolve the wax, putting the receptacle into a basin containing boiling water; never heat such mixtures over a naked flame as they are inflammable. When the waxes have dissolved, pour the mixture into the distilled water/soap solution and allow it to cool for twenty-four hours, when it will be ready for use. Stir the mixture before applying it with a lint-free soft cloth; it acts both as a reviver and a polish.

◇ BLEACHING ◇

Bleaching can be done successfully if you first study its limitations, as not all woods can be bleached effectively, even after a couple of applications. Here is a list of the bleaching capabilities of some popular timbers:

Ash: bleaches easily, usually after one application.
Avodire: as ash.
Basswood: not suitable.
Beech: as ash.
Birch: as ash.
Cherry: not suitable.
Chestnut: not suitable.
Ebony: not suitable.
Elm: as ash.
Iroko: not suitable.

Mahoganies: probably two applications needed.
Maple: as ash.
Oaks: as mahoganies.
Padauk: not suitable.
Pine: not suitable.
Poplar: as mahoganies.
Rosewood: not suitable.
Satinwood: not suitable.
Walnut: as mahoganies.

There are, of course, proprietary bleaches and we strongly recommend you to use one of them, particularly if you are dealing with a large area. Usually they are two-part, the first being alkali and the second hydrogen peroxide; after the first liquid is applied the wood may darken in tone but this is nothing to worry about as it is simply preparing the wood surface for the chemical reaction which takes place when the second part is applied. As with all proprietary products, follow the manufacturers' instructions exactly. When handling bleach, wear strong gloves and old clothes; wash away any splashes on your skin or in your eyes with copious amounts of water; and do not put the bleach in any metallic container, as metal will react with it.

It is most likely that you have to contend with bleaching out spots and small patches. Before starting, get rid of greasy finger-marks with a grease-remover as they will, of course, resist the bleach. Do not take it for granted that there aren't any because they are not obvious; it is usually worthwhile degreasing any part that gets handled frequently – knobs and the area around a lock are two examples. Put the bleach on with a brush or sponge; choose a cheap throwaway brush as bleach is hard on bristles. The bleach should be allowed to dry on the surface until the desired appearance is achieved; the manufacturers' instructions will tell you whether the bleach should be rinsed off, or neutralised. Once the bleached area is dry, rub it down very lightly to remove any 'whiskers' of raised grain; do not overdo it as the bleach does not penetrate very far into the wood. It is worth allowing at least forty-eight hours for the bleach to dry, as insufficient drying time can cause bubbles to appear later after the area has been polished.

As an alternative to proprietary wood bleaches you could try one of the following:

1 Oxalic acid. Dissolve 25g (1oz) of the powder, or 50g (2oz) of the crystals in 600ml (1pt) of very hot water. Brush the solution on while it is hot and let it remain for fifteen minutes or so before wiping it off with a damp cloth. If the result is unsatisfactory, repeat the procedure. Then neutralise the bleach by washing it off with a solution of 1 part of ammonia to 10 parts of water, followed by a rinse with plain water, and allow it to dry. An alternative neutraliser is 25g (1oz) borax to 1.2 litres (1 quart) of warm water.

2 Hydrogen peroxide on its own. This is the 100-vol grade which is used commercially, not the very diluted grade used as an antiseptic. It does not need to be neutralised.

3 Household bleaches. These are comparatively mild, but come in useful for 'spotting'; they can be neutralised by rinsing with plain water after fifteen minutes or so.

◇ STAINS AND STAINING ◇

The purpose of staining is to produce uniformity of colour and tone and to enhance the natural beauty of the grain; it also helps to match in a replacement piece to its surround. All the stains discussed here are transparent and do not conceal the grain in any way.

Water stains

These come in two forms: as aniline dye powders which have to be dissolved; or ready-mixed. Both kinds are cheap and can be freely mixed to make any colour. Additionally, they have good spreading and penetrative qualities and give clear, definite colours with no muddiness. They can be applied with a piece of canvas, a large brush or, preferably, with a spray gun.

Unfortunately, they have one distinct disadvantage in that they raise the grain and, once it is dry, the stained surface has to be glasspapered to get rid of the 'whiskers' etc. If you are not very careful this glasspapering can remove the stain in patches and result in a streaked appearance. You can minimise the risk by raising the grain before the stain is applied by going over the piece with a wet cloth, allowing the surface to dry, and glasspapering it. Although this treatment will not entirely stop the grain from rising after staining it will certainly help to reduce it.

To prepare the stain, heat 4.5 litres (1gal) of water to just below boiling point in a container (which can be any metal other than aluminium or copper) and add 100g (4oz) of the aniline powder, stirring all the while. When it is cool, store it in glass bottles which have corks or non-metallic stoppers; it will remain usable indefinitely and can be diluted to choice. If the water in your district is very hard or contains chemicals, play safe and use distilled water.

If you are applying the stain by brush or rag you need to work fast as the stain dries quickly; you must keep a 'live' edge as once the edge has dried it will appear as a streak. Always work along the grain, as if a streak does form it will be much less noticeable than if it runs across the grain; also, always work from an edge with strokes running the full length – if you start from the middle of, say, a panel you will have two edges to worry about instead of one.

End grain is a problem as it soaks up stain like a sponge and can entirely spoil the appearance. To cope with this, have a small amount of the stain in a separate container and dilute it so that it is lighter in tone and you have some control of its effect on end grain.

If possible, arrange to have the work lying horizontal while you stain it, but do hold it up in its final position from time to time. The reason for doing this is because vertical pieces always appear darker than horizontal ones (see Fig 46), and you will be able to correct this by applying more stain to the horizontals.

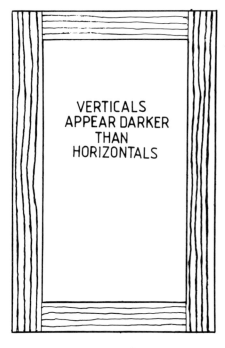

VERTICALS APPEAR DARKER THAN HORIZONTALS

Fig 46

While the surface is still wet go over the work with a lint-free cloth which has been moistened with stain to pick up any surplus and make the surface as uniform in colour as possible.

Using a spray gun should reduce the likelihood of streaks as you can regulate accurately the amount of stain being applied. You will, of course, need to mask off the areas near to the part being sprayed, and large pieces of cardboard are handy for this.

There are several recipes for homemade water stains:

1 Bichromate of potash. This comes in the form of reddish-orange crystals which are steeped in water until dissolved; the solution can then be diluted as required. It only affects certain timbers such as mahoganies and oaks; it will not act on pine. Genuine Cuban and Spanish mahoganies become deep red, while Honduras and other West African mahoganies tend to take on a rather cold dark brown shade. On brown oaks, the colour becomes darker with a greenish tinge, and on white (light coloured) oaks it gives a rich brown.

2 Sulphate of iron, also known as 'green copperas'. It comes in the form of crystals which have to be dissolved in water at the proportion of 1 teaspoonful to 600ml (1pt) of water. This will give a greenish solution. It can be used to kill the redness of mahogany so that it will resemble walnut; it will also turn sycamore to a grey colour and this is the well-known 'harewood'. Sulphate of iron turns other woods grey or grey-blue as well, including ash, beech, birch, chestnut, oak and obeche, but none of them is very attractive. Be careful to dilute it when you use it as if it is too strong you will get a muddy grey tone.

3 Permanganate of potash is another stain that is sometimes recommended. Again, it is sold as crystals which, when dissolved in warm water become a rich purple solution; a finger dipped into it will acquire an instant brown suntan! Unfortunately the effect on wood is fugitive and fades in a comparatively short time.

Oil stains

These contain dye dissolved in turpentine, or naphtha, or similar oils, and can be freely mixed with each other; they are available in a wide range of colours and have the advantage that they do not raise the grain. They can be applied with a brush or a rag and you will not have to worry too much about keeping a live edge, but they tend to give a flat, muddy colour.

One point to note, however, is that if you contemplate using a wax polish afterwards the stain should be fixed with a couple of coats of clear (white) French polish. If this is not done, the wax polish may lift up the stain in patches as they may have the same solvent.

Spirit stains

These are not widely used as they are difficult to apply. The stain dries out rapidly and it is almost impossible to keep a live edge. They can be sprayed, however, and this solves the problem. If the solvent is methylated spirits do not use any finish which contains it or the stain may be picked up. However, as they will penetrate a varnish finish, spirit stains are handy for touching up small patches and will dry in a quarter of an hour or so; unless well protected by finishing coats the colour may fade if exposed to strong light.

Wax stains

These can be used if you want to tone the wood to a different shade, although normally wax polish is applied to a natural timber. Apply them freely and allow them thirty-six hours or so to dry and for all the solvent to evaporate; until this has happened you will not be able to obtain a sheen.

◇ SEALERS AND FILLERS ◇

As soon as a stain has dried, the stained surface should be sealed. This prevents the stain from bleeding into subsequent coats, and it also seals the pores ready for either a filler or for the final polishing.

We recommend that you apply as a sealer a thin coat of whatever finish you intend to use, and it should be so sparse that there is no 'shine'. So for varnish finishes (except synthetic lacquers which do not specify a solvent) thin the varnish 50/50 with turpentine or turpentine substitute. For French polish dilute 1 part clear polish with 8 parts of methylated spirits. Once the sealer has dried, glasspaper off any nibs or roughness before applying the filler; if you are not going to use a filler but intend to proceed with the final coat, you will have to take more care and smooth the surface perfectly.

Filling the grain is not obligatory but a matter of personal choice. Some timbers, such as ash, chestnut, oak and teak, have open grain with large 'pores', and fillers are used to provide a smooth gloss finish. But the same result can be achieved by using polish or varnish alone; it will just take more time and more polish. Paste fillers are sold in various colours to match the basic colours of wood and these are usually red, brown and natural. They can be thinned with best quality turpentine substitute and are applied with a rag either before or after staining; in fact, if you do not want to colour the wood too much you can dispense with stain altogether and rely on the coloured filler alone. It is important to note that if you intend to use a synthetic lacquer as a finish you must use a paste filler that is compatible with the varnish – the manufacturers' instructions usually recommend a suitable filler.

Techniques of varnishing and lacquering
Properly done, this is one of the best finishes; to apply it correctly does not involve any mysteries but does demand patience, cleanliness, and attention to a few basic rules.

The varnishes discussed here include the traditional oil varnishes (the only ones which should be used for restoration) and the modern synthetic lacquers; the methods employed are the same for all except that the oil varnish needs at least twenty-four hours to dry, but it can then be rubbed back equally as well as the synthetics.

As mentioned earlier in this chapter, oil varnish ingredients are natural resins or gums with linseed oil or tung oil as a vehicle plus a thinner such as turpentine to render the varnish workable. The synthetic resins, however, contain alkyds, formaldehydes, phenols, vinyls and urethanes; combinations of these resins give different qualities to the lacquer, and the principal classifications are as follows:

1 Cabinet lacquer. This contains proportionately more resins than oil and is a general-purpose varnish which can be used on all interior work. It is easy to apply and responds to rubbing to give a high gloss. Like all synthetic resins it is impervious to water spillage, alcohol, oil and grease, and withstands accidental knocks and scratches.
2 Matt lacquer. This dries with a dull, semi-gloss surface and should be applied over a cabinet varnish if you want this type of finish. It needs no rubbing.
3 Interior spar varnish. This is formulated for surfaces which have to withstand constant hard usage, such as café tables, bar counters, etc. It can be rubbed to give a fairly good satin gloss.
4 Rubbing varnish. The one to use if you want a gloss-hard surface which can be rubbed to achieve a really smooth and lustrous finish.
5 Polyurethane UVA lacquer. This has an ingredient which prevents the finish fading when exposed to strong sunlight – UVA means 'ultra-violet absorbing'. It has all the qualities of cabinet varnish and can be rubbed to a high finish.

The colouring effect varies slightly – thus, urethanes and vinyls are the clearest and hardly tint the wood surface, while phenolic lacquers tend to yellow; alkyds are usually clear if bought from a reputable manufacturer.

The conditions for applying all varnishes, both oil and synthetic, are the same and must be adhered to if you want the best results. The

Fig 47

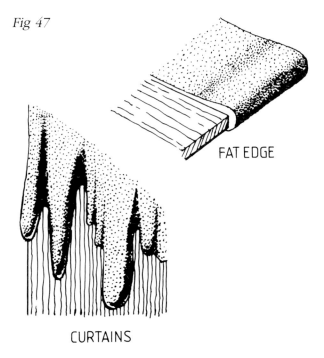

FAT EDGE

CURTAINS

particles – just sprinkle a few drops of the varnish you are using on to some lint-free cloth and rub them in so that the cloth becomes tacky. If you can avoid it, do not varnish during damp weather and of course, make sure the wood is bone-dry.

Use a proper varnish brush which has longer and more supple bristles than an ordinary paint brush. If it is a new one, clean it by soaking the bristles in turpentine substitute (white spirit) and then knead the bristles in your fingers to get rid of loose hairs and dust. Never use the brush for anything but varnish. A good way to store it is shown in Fig 48 – the lid reduces evaporation of the turpentine substitute solvent, and the wire through the handle of the brush prevents the tips of the bristles bending against the bottom of the tin.

ambient temperature is critical and should be about 21°C (70°F); under 18°C (65°F) is too cold and the varnish will not flow freely, and over 26°C (80°F) it will do the opposite and flow too readily with consequent risks of 'curtains' and 'fat' edges. 'Curtains' is the term used to describe the sagging overflow shown in Fig 47, while a 'fat' edge refers to the excessive build-up at an edge.

Dust that settles on the varnish while it is drying is one of your principal enemies and you can take some simple measures to control it. Sweep the floor and dampen it to prevent dust rising; keep the door shut but have some air coming through a partly-open window; do not wear clothing which harbours dust; make yourself a 'tack rag' which will pick up dust and other

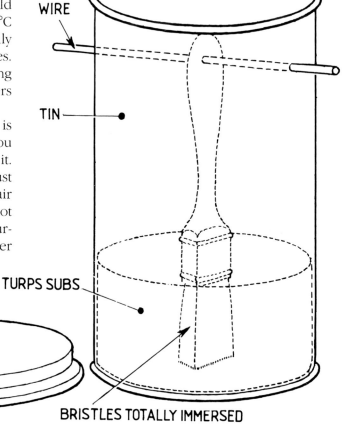

WIRE

TIN

TURPS SUBS

LID

BRISTLES TOTALLY IMMERSED

Fig 48

Before you begin applying the varnish it is worth going to some trouble to arrange for the work to be horizontal (to avoid runs, curtains, etc), with the light directly in front of you. Start by applying a sealing coat, which should be 1 part varnish as it comes from the tin to an equal part of thinner (turpentine substitute or whatever the manufacturer specifies). Be very careful not to introduce any air bubbles either into the tin of varnish or into the varnish film as you apply it; use as large a brush as is practicable and dip it into the varnish slowly and gently so that the bristles are comfortably full to about half their length. You do not brush out varnish as you do with paint, but flow it on first *across the grain,* then dry the brush and draw the bristle tips lightly *along the grain.*

If you have too much varnish on the brush, or if you want almost to dry the brush, it is not a good idea to squeeze or drag the bristles against the rim of the can as you will introduce air bubbles. It is far better to tie a piece of string across a glass jar (Fig 49) and draw the bristles across it; you can eventually return the excess varnish back to the main tin once the air bubbles have disappeared. Drawing or stroking the almost-dry bristles across the varnished surface will help to work out any runs, curtains, or fat edges.

When applying the varnish, start with an area about 205mm (8in) square and work from the centre outwards so that you do not wipe the bristles over an edge – this is the most likely cause of a fat edge. Other faults which often appear are:

1 Sweating. This occurs when varnish is rubbed before it is thoroughly dry.
2 Pinholes. Usually caused by the varnish being applied on a damp surface, or because the thinner was not mixed properly with the varnish.
3 Crawling. Frequently the result of coats being too thick, or of atmospheric changes.
4 Crackling. This is a kind of crazing which is often seen on old pieces, and is caused by applying one grade of varnish over a different one with the result that the two have varying degrees of elasticity – it normally takes a comparatively long time to develop.

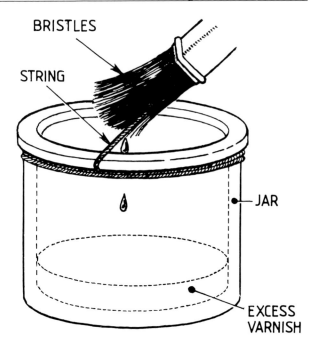

Fig 49

5 Blooming. This is a cloudiness in the film caused by the varnish being applied in too damp an atmosphere.

The drying times of different brands of proprietary varnishes can vary and it is essential to follow the manufacturer's instructions carefully. Some varnishes are ready for a second coat only *between* 4 and 8 hours or *after* 48 hours – due to evaporation of the solvents a second coat will not bond well between 8 and 48 hours. (After 48 hours the first coat will need to be glasspapered lightly to form a key for the second coat.) If there are no manufacturer's instructions it is advisable to leave at least 48 hours between coats.

Papering down the sealing coat can be done with superfine 'flour' glasspaper used dry and very lightly rubbed along the grain. Remove the dust with your tack tag. For the following coats (except the last one) use the finest grade of wet-and-dry paper lubricated with soapy water; rinse the sludge off with clean water and dry with a chamois leather and a soft cloth. Again, paper in the direction of the grain.

Having left the final coat for four or five days to dry (curing would be a better description, as the so-called drying is actually a chemical reaction), you can start the final rubbing down to achieve a lustrous finish. You need some pumice powder of the finest grade, a piece of 6mm (¼in) thick felt about 75mm (3in) square, and a lubricant which can be light machine oil of the type used for sewing machines, typewriters, etc. Pour some of the oil into a shallow container (a tin lid will do) and dip the felt pad into it and then into the pumice powder. Rub with a moderate pressure along the grain in long even strokes from end to end; from time to time wipe away the sludge to examine the finish, which should acquire a satin-like appearance. Finally, wipe off the sludge with a soft clean rag in the direction of the grain.

If you want to attain a really lustrous high polish, the next step is to leave the pumice-oil-rubbed surface to harden for a week or so, and then rub it down with rottenstone powder and water. The method is the same as already described, ie a felt pad is dipped in water and then rottenstone and rubbed in the direction of the grain, followed by a final wipe with a soft rag.

Oil finishes

Oil finishes comprise (a) the application of linseed oil; and (b) the use of specially formulated oils such as teak oil and Danish oil.

Dealing with (a) first, the linseed oil can be either raw or boiled, and can be heated before application. This heating can be accomplished safely by standing the oil container in another one with boiling water in it and simmering (not boiling) the oil for about fifteen minutes. Then add turpentine substitute in the proportion of 1 part to 8 parts of linseed oil: if you introduce terebene (drier) at the rate of one teaspoonful to half a pint of the mixture, it will help it to dry.

While the mixture is still warm, apply it to the wood with a lint-free rag and then rub vigorously along the grain with a piece of soft cloth or felt wrapped around a house brick. The brick helps you to apply pressure as it is the rubbing that matters; not for nothing is it called the 'elbow grease' polish! Even after several repeat performances, you still won't have worked up much of a shine but this will eventually come if you give it a rubbing with the mixture every month or so; in fact, the surface will always take more oil and

more friction provided you allow it to dry out for a week or two between applications.

Teak oil (or Danish oil, as it is sometimes called) is a flat finish with very little sheen or body and was formulated for the present-day Scandinavian styles of furniture, where the aim is to permit the grain of the wood to be its own adornment. It is simply brushed on, allowed to soak in, then wiped off. You can incorporate colour if you wish into either the first or second coat, but never into the final coat, which must be clear. Simply get some artists' oil pigments and mix them in a small quantity of the oil to the colour you want and then brush it into the finish while it is still wet.

Wax polishes

Wax polishes are deservedly popular as they are straightforward to apply and impart a glowing sheen to the wood once you have invested enough energy and time to bring up the shine. It will not, of course, resist spilt liquids or cups of hot tea, but a clock is rarely in a position to be at risk from them!

You can apply a wax polish over water stains or oil stain but your first step *must* be to apply one, or preferably two, coats of clear French polish to the work. This seals the grain so that dust and dirt cannot enter. Obviously, constant polishing over the years must deposit some grime, and the French polish prevents it being rubbed into the grain; when the wax gets dirty after many years you can remove it and start again with a clean surface. The sealer will also stop the turpentine in the wax polish pulling off patches of oil stain, which often has turpentine or turpentine substitute as a solvent. If you do use oil stain, rub over the job with a piece of coarse rag or canvas to get rid of any traces of grease; you can then apply the French polish sealer.

The main ingredients of a good home-made wax polish are beeswax, carnauba wax and best quality turpentine substitute. Beeswax comes in two colours: raw or unbleached, which is a medium-brown colour and is suitable for medium to dark woods; or bleached, which is a straw colour and suitable for light woods. For antique polish you can add lamp-black powder colour. If you want a wax that will fill the grain immediately, mix in some cornflour – it will delay the arrival of the sheen until the filler has dried out but you will be able to buff it up eventually.

Both waxes should be shredded (a nutmeg grater is ideal for this job) and the amounts should be equal. Put the carnauba in a saucepan and just cover it with the turpentine substitute – it needs warming to help the wax dissolve. Do not put the saucepan directly on to a naked flame as the mixture is inflammable; put the pan into a larger one which contains hot water and keep the water simmering until the wax dissolves – stirring now and again will help. Take the pan off and add more turpentine substitute until the volume in the pan has doubled, and then sprinkle in the beeswax. This should dissolve readily but you may need to return the pan to the hot water.

The result, when cool, should be a paste; if it is too hard, melt it (again over a pan of hot water) and add more turpentine substitute; if it is too sloppy, melt it and add more wax. The ideal consistency of the paste is that of toothpaste. You apply it to the wood by scrubbing it into the grain fairly generously with a stiff-bristled brush such as a shoe-brush. Then leave the job alone for at least twenty-four hours for the wax to dry, when you can go over it with another brush, followed by buffing-up with a lint-free cloth. You may have to repeat the whole procedure until the wax is spread evenly, but once this has been attained, regular polishing with a soft cloth and a smear of the wax should keep the surface in good condition.

If you do not want to bother with making your own polish there are some excellent proprietary waxes on the market which will produce a perfect finish if you follow the manufacturers' instructions.

6 Gilding

Gilding is a craft in its own right (some would say an art) which requires a lifetime's experience to perfect. It is important to know one's limitations, as trying to be too ambitious can lead to disaster. We restrict our advice here to ways of dealing with the simpler problems.

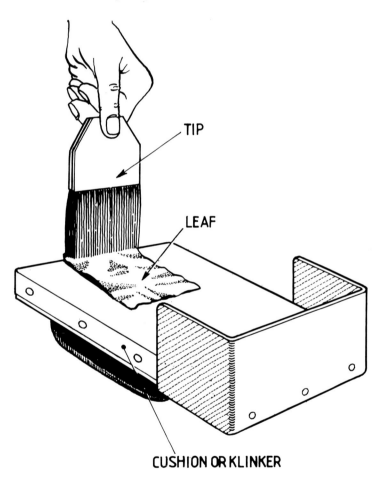

TIP

LEAF

CUSHION OR KLINKER

◇ REPAIRS TO GILDING ◇

First of all, we must make it clear that the gilding discussed here relates to wood (covered with gesso) and not to metalwork, which is treated in an entirely different way; this is a distinction not always appreciated by those who deal in antiques. Carved wood which has been covered with gesso is always covered with gold leaf, but metalwork was 'fire-gilt' in the old days by a process which is now obsolete and illegal, and today it is either gold-lacquered or electroplated.

For small imperfections you can use wax gilt, which can be bought from most art shops; it comes in several tones of gold. It is easy to apply as you can spread and smooth it on to flat surfaces with your finger or a pad of soft cloth; use a fairly stiff brush to get it into crevices on carved pieces.

A better method on comparatively small areas is to use a mixture consisting of a teaspoonful of quick-drying size with a quarter-teaspoonful of gold powder. If the mixture has brown streaks on the surface it is an indication that the mixture has too high a proportion of size, and a pinch of gold powder needs to be added and mixed in. Quick-drying size can be obtained from suppliers of gilding material. Buy it in small quantities as it gels quickly in large quantities – you can guard against this by adding two or three drops of turpentine (preferably pure turpentine and not white spirit) after use, and keeping the can tightly closed.

Gold powders are, in fact, made from bronze and come in different shades; you may need to tint the one you have to match the existing gilding. To do this, place a dab of each of the 'earth' colours in the separate troughs of a watercolour-painting china palette; these colours are burnt sienna, burnt umber, raw sienna, raw umber and yellow ochre. The yellow ochre and raw sienna give a yellowish tint; the burnt sienna a warm reddish brown; the two umbers impart a brown colour. A drop of 'flatting oil' (1 part boiled linseed mixed with 6 parts white spirit) will help to bind the colour to the gold powder mixture.

Apply the final mixture to the work with a brush, very much as if you were painting a picture, and allow it to dry. It will then need some form of protection; best quality clear shellac is good for this. If you want the gold to assume a tawny hue, use orange shellac instead of clear. Remember, however, that you cannot burnish the surface.

Both wax gilt and bronze powders tend to tarnish after a few months, even if sealed after application, so are not suitable for large areas.

◇ GILDING LARGE AREAS ◇

When gilding comparatively large areas and ornamental carving the first point to consider is the primary difference between the two methods which can be used, namely water gilding and oil gilding. In water gilding, as its name implies, the gold leaf is laid on to the work after the latter has been moistened with water; the resulting finish can be burnished to a beautiful sheen. Oil gilding, on the other hand, cannot be burnished and is laid in conjunction with the gold size. There is no reason why you should not combine the two methods on different areas of the same piece, using water gilding for the burnished flat areas and highlights, and oil gilding on the delicate convolutions of carved parts. Both techniques are explained fully later in the chapter, but first we must discuss the materials used prior to gilding.

◇ COMPO AND GESSO ◇

Let us assume that you have made a new clock and would like to enrich its appearance with some gilt ornament; it could be carved and gilt moulding or a more elaborate carved cresting on the hood. You can tackle this in one of two ways, either by means of 'compo' or by 'gesso' laid over carved wood.

Compo was invented by the Adams brothers in the eighteenth century and they made great use of it on furniture, mirror and picture frames, and fire surrounds. The recipe for it is as follows. Boil 450g (1lb) Scotch glue in 300ml (½pt) of water. Then add about 200g (7oz) of white resin to 300ml (½pt) of raw linseed oil and mix them together in a separate container; take the glue and water mixture off the heat and add the resin and linseed oil to it. Put the receptacle containing the mixture into a larger one which has boiling water in it so that you have a double-boiler and return it to the heat. Let it boil for half an hour; give it a stir from time to time and then allow it to cool until it is lukewarm. Tip it on to a bed of gilders' whiting or kaolin powder. The kaolin will make the compo a grey colour but this does not matter; knead it until it resembles dough, when it can be used. It tends to harden when stored but can be softened by being placed on a piece of linen which has been tied over the top of a pan of boiling water – the steam will make it malleable. The compo can be shaped with modelling tools such as those used for Plasticine, and when it has set hard it can be carved.

One of the principal advantages of compo is that it is comparatively inexpensive and therefore ideal for large work, but it is undoubtedly messy and time-consuming to prepare. As an alternative, you might like to try an epoxy putty which is made up from epoxy resin adhesive with kaolin powder mixed into it. The epoxy adhesive is quite expensive, so it is not economical for large work, but it is ideal for small stuff. You can get kaolin cheaply from most chemists, and it makes a putty which is not sticky and very pliable. But from the point of view of conservation you should use traditional compo for restoration work.

Epoxy resin adhesives come in two parts, one tube being the adhesive, and the other tube containing the hardener. The adhesive has a critical setting time and is available in two types: quick setting, and slow setting. For our purposes we need the slow setting one. Mix up the putty on a piece of broken glass (which can be thrown away after use); follow the manufacturers' instructions, which are usually to squeeze out equal amounts side by side from each tube and then to mix them thoroughly. The kaolin is sprinkled on and mixed in at the same time; after a time, the length of which depends on the surrounding temperature, the mixture will assume a consistency like soft toffee and this is the state in which you can model it. Tools used for modelling (including your fingers) can be cleaned with methylated spirit or surgical spirit; once the putty begins really to harden off you can use acetone as a solvent but once it has set completely there seems to be no solvent.

Compo and epoxy putty are suitable for use with moulds so that if you want to repair a symmetrical or repeating pattern of ornament you can take a mould from an undamaged portion and cast a replacement piece. Epoxy resin can be used to repair broken ormolu work (see Chapter 4). Moulding material can be a proprietary brand such as Vinamould (from craft shops), or the brown gum called Paribar which dentists use for taking moulds for dentures. The latter is simple to use and can be softened in hot water, but beware of leaving it in hot water over a flame as when it is heated beyond its softening point it turns into a liquid and will become a sticky mess on the bottom of the container. Once softened it can be pressed over whatever has to be copied, left for a minute or so and then removed with a knife blade dipped in hot water. You should not need a release agent but if you are in doubt, because the pattern to be copied is very intricate, a light smear of Vaseline will suffice. Paribar can be obtained from dental technicians (look in the Yellow Pages telephone directory) and you will not need much as it can be used time after time. Both compo and epoxy putty patterns can be glued into position; use Scotch glue or a PVA woodworking adhesive for the compo, and an epoxy resin adhesive for the putty.

Now we come to gesso, the material used by gilders over the centuries as a groundwork for laying gold leaf which is to be burnished. It is essential for success in gilding.

First of all, obtain (from gilders' suppliers) some parchment cuttings – 225g (8oz) or so would be a good quantity to start with. After cutting them into strips an inch or so long put them into a plastic bowl, add cold water to cover them well (as they will absorb it) and leave them to soak overnight. Next morning, strain off any surplus water, put the cuttings into an ovenware bowl and add cold water to approximately three times their volume. Place the bowl into a saucepan of boiling water and keep it simmering for three or four hours; then strain it through a hair sieve or an old nylon stocking into another receptacle. Let it cool and coagulate. The degree of gelling is all-important – it should resemble a dessert jelly and if you hit the jug with your hand, it should break up (the jelly not the jug!). If it is too hard, add a little water, warm up the jelly and let it cool before testing it again; it is all a matter of trial and error. What you have made is called 'parchment size'; there are other recipes and methods but this is the most reliable one.

To convert this gesso size into actual gesso you need to warm up the size again and gradually add gilders' whiting, stirring all the time and pressing out any lumps against the side of the receptacle; the aim is to get a mixture of the consistency of ready-mixed paint. Finally, stir in a couple of drops of linseed oil and then strain the mixture again through a hair sieve or a nylon stocking; you will probably have to push it through with a blunt-pointed piece of wood but this does not matter – the primary considerations are to get rid of any lumps, even tiny specks, and to ensure that the size and the whiting are thoroughly mixed.

◇ WATER GILDING ON WOOD ◇

This is the method to use for a burnished finish and first you have to apply at least six, preferably eight, coats of gesso; they have to be completed in one session, allowing each coat to dry before applying the next. Do not attempt to speed the drying with artificial heat as you could cause a skin to form on the outside. The moral is to make up enough gesso beforehand, as it must be freshly mixed.

Keep the container with the gesso in a pan of hot water to prevent it setting and apply a thin coat with a good hog-hair, or ox-hair, flat brush. While this is drying (this takes about one hour per coat in normal conditions) have a look at the work and check it for knots, open joints (particularly at mitres), and any splits or cracks. These should be masked with strips of silk or fine linen cut amply to cover the defect; each strip should be dipped into the gesso and stretched tautly in place before the second coat is applied.

Be careful when loading the brush not to introduce any air bubbles which would eventually burst and cause pinholes; if you have too much gesso on your brush, wipe the excess off carefully on a piece of spare wood. It is a good idea, too, to apply the gesso in alternate vertical and horizontal coats if the shape of the work allows it. Be careful to avoid any build-up in crevices as these frequently crack when the gesso dries. If you find that the gesso has run down into a crevice and formed a thick deposit, remove the excess with a piece of dampened linen wrapped around a stick – the sticks used for children's ice-lollies are suitable if cut to shape.

Ideally, the coats of gesso should be so smooth that they do not need glasspapering but, life being what it is, you will probably have to do it. Wait until the gesso is completely dry and then rub it very lightly with the finest flour-paper grade of glasspaper; in fact, it is worth rubbing two sheets of the paper against each other to make them even smoother. At this juncture you can, if necessary, get out your carving tools and sharpen up the contours and details of any carved work. But it is a moot point whether it is advisable or not, as it is difficult to burnish gold leaf laid on sharp edges without removing it, so a slight rounding-off is not only acceptable, but beneficial.

Applying the bole

Next you have to lay on three or four coats of Armenian bole, which is a special clay that imparts a dark red surface to the gesso. It can be burnished with a piece of linen to a mirror finish which will not only accept and hold the gold leaf but will also enhance the colour of the gold.

You can buy the bole from a gilders' supplier, but you will have to mix it with some of the parchment size described above. The size should be diluted to the extent of its own volume with cold water, and the best way to do this is to warm the size and stir in the water gradually, followed by the bole, until it is the consistency of thin cream. It will, of course, have to be strained through a fine strainer so that it is completely free from any lumps, however small.

Put the first coat on with a fairly stiff brush, but use a softer one for the ensuing two or three coats – each coat must be allowed to dry before applying the next; then leave the work to dry completely for at least twelve hours. Your great enemy now is dust, so make sure the surroundings are as dust-free as possible. It is advisable to arrange some kind of a tent or cover for the work while it dries.

When drying is complete you may need to remove nibs or specks of bole or dust from the surface before burnishing; do this by means of a light papering with the finest flour-grade glasspaper. The final result should be a highly polished, totally smooth, dark red surface which is the prerequisite for a first-class burnished finish.

It is worth mentioning here that you may be able to obtain cones of ready-mixed burnishing clay which are ideal for small repair jobs. All you need to do is to moisten a brush and rub it on to the cone; the resulting paste is painted on to the area to be repaired.

◇ OIL GILDING ON WOOD ◇

Oil gilding, which cannot satisfactorily be burnished, is used for areas that are to be left matt.

The simplest method is to dispense with the gesso and bole altogether and paint the wood with, first, a coat of pink primer, followed by two coats of yellow undercoat (or as many coats as are necessary to obliterate the grain) and, finally, a coat of gloss paint which should be as close to the colour of yellow ochre (a brownish yellow) as possible. Remove any nibs with flour glasspaper, then apply a coat of gold size, and you are ready to lay the gold.

There is another method which will produce good results, although it is rather more complicated. It involves preparing the groundwork as if for water gilding, but using only two or three coats of gesso to fill the grain, and then following this by applying a coat of yellow clay (from gilders' suppliers); the clay is mixed in just the same way as described for the Armenian bole. If

the surface needs it, use the finest grade glasspaper to remove any nibs or irregularities, dust away any debris and apply two coats of clear size (this consists of 1 part ordinary glue size to 2 parts warm water).

When the size has dried, the next job is to brush on a coat of eighteen-hour gold size; eighteen hours is the approximate time taken by the size to become tacky and in the right condition to accept the gold leaf. Make sure that all parts have been covered by a thin film of the gold size as you must avoid 'holidays' (areas which have been missed) and puddles on the high spots and in the crevices. It is worth while making some kind of protective covering to prevent dust sticking to the size as it can ruin the surface. From time to time test to see if the size is in the right condition of tackiness; when you touch it lightly with your finger and feel it pulling it should be ready.

◇ GOLD LEAF ◇

We must emphasise that working with gold leaf is one of the most difficult crafts to master as it takes years of practice to become thoroughly accomplished. However, there is no reason why you should not attain enough proficiency to turn out a satisfactory job. If you can obtain some aluminium or Dutch gold leaf (an alloy of copper and zinc), you can use it to practise with; admittedly they are both heavier than gold leaf but at least you would learn the basic handling techniques.

Equipment

The tools needed are listed below and shown in Figs 50A–H. Some of them you can make for yourself; the remainder can be obtained from a gilders' supplier:

(A) The gilder's cushion, or 'klinker', on which the leaf is laid for manipulation. You can make this yourself. Cut a piece of wood or, better still, multi-plywood (which will not warp) about 255×153mm (10×6in) by 12mm (½in) thick. Then cut three pieces of good-quality flannel to this size and lay them on the wood, covering them with a piece of genuine chamois stretched taut and tacked in place around the edges. Nail on some pieces of buckram or stiff parchment, as shown, to act as a wind-shield against draughts; make it about 64mm (2½in) high. Then tack on a leather loop to the underside so that you can put your thumb through it and hold the cushion like an artist's palette. Finally, sprinkle some French chalk on to the cushion and rub it in well with the flat side of the gilder's knife – this will help to keep the cushion free from grease.

(B) The gilder's knife. It is best to buy one, although you might be able to adapt one from the cutlery drawer. It needs to be longer than an ordinary table knife, with a blade 178–203mm (7–8in) long which is slightly flexible and parallel from heel to tip, and with the tip ground at an angle of 45 degrees; another feature is that it has a fairly blunt edge. The blade must be kept highly polished with rouge paper (obtainable from jewellers) so that the gold leaf will not adhere to it and tatter.

(C) The burnisher. The best ones are polished agate mounted on wooden handles; some have metal handles but are tiring to work with. In ancient times they used a dog's tooth, so if you are a veterinary surgeon you are in luck! You must break in a new agate burnisher by polishing it on a piece of felt impregnated with linseed oil and rottenstone; whenever you use a burnisher it should be warmed up first by being rubbed with a piece of felt.

(D) The gilder's tip, used to carry the leaf from the cushion to the work. Obtained from gilders' suppliers. It consists of hairs sandwiched between two 102mm (4in) wide pieces of cardboard. To straighten the hairs, lay the tip on a flat surface with the side of your hand pressing it down firmly; then, with the other hand, pull the tip out and repeat the process, having first turned the tip over so that the hairs are flattened from each side.

(E) The gilder's mop. This is a No 3 camel-hair brush with (preferably) a wooden handle, and is used to apply the water-gesso solution which is the vehicle for the gold leaf.

(F) Lining brush, used to position the leaf on the work. This is the kind of brush employed by sign-writers; you want one with 38mm (1½in) bristles mounted in a quill; this quill should be fitted on to the end of the mop (E), hence the wooden handle, which may have to be shaped to fit.

(G) A small ovenware bowl or 'pipkin' to contain the water-gesso solution referred to in (E).

(H) The tamper. A flat 25mm (1in) wide brush with ox-hair or hog-hair bristles which is used for 'skewing' (brushing away excess of gold leaf).

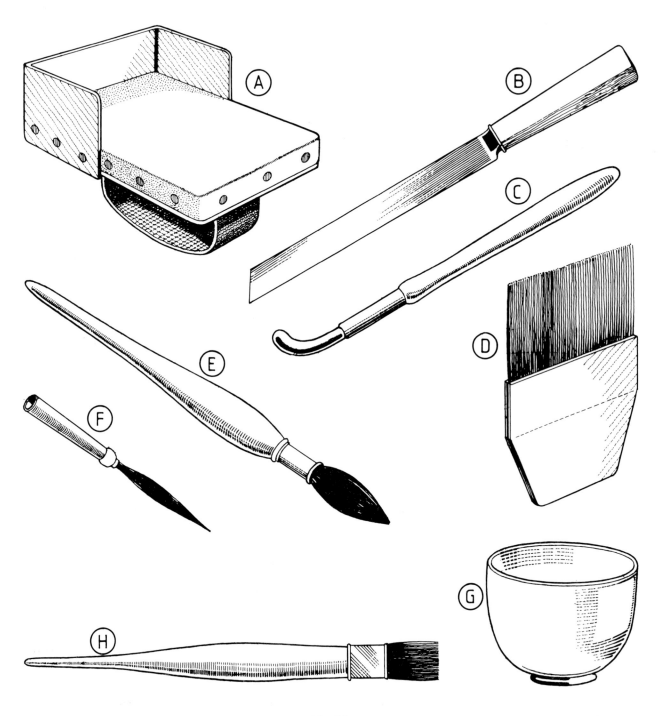

Fig 50

Types of gold leaf

Gold leaf comes in the form of a thin paper 'book' consisting of twenty-five leaves, each 82mm (3¼in) square; a hundred such books constitute a pack (in the USA, twenty books are a pack). You need what is called 'loose leaf'; the other kind available is 'transfer gold' which means that the leaf is attached to tissue paper by a wax film. This is for exterior work and although it can be used for our purposes, the gold tends to cling to the wax film, leaving gaps in the gilding.

Gold leaf is offered in various colours which are achieved by adding small quantities of silver or copper; pure gold is not malleable enough to be beaten into the exquisite thinness of gold leaf. The smaller the carat content is, the more likely the leaf is to tarnish. As a guide, lemon gold is 18½ carats; pale gold 16 carats; and white gold 12 carats.

Working with gold leaf

For some reason, probably because gold is highly susceptible to static electricity, the best conditions for working with gold leaf are when the temperature is about 21°C (70°F) and the atmosphere is reasonably moist – hot, dry weather makes the job more difficult.

Before opening the book of leaves, have all your tools within easy reach. Also have ready the vehicle for laying the leaves, which is prepared by dissolving one tablespoon of the parchment size as used for the gesso (see page 74) into a cupful of distilled water; this should be poured into an ovenproof bowl which is placed in a container of hot water to warm it while you stir it thoroughly. The resulting solution must, however, be used cold and not while it is still warm.

Open the book of leaves and use the knife to move a leaf on to the front of the cushion. This is easier said than done, and you may find the best way is to cut off the spine of the book with a pair of scissors and then remove the covers and the top tissue. Place the book upside down on the front of the cushion and use the knife and your fingers to remove all the book except the bottom leaf; put the remainder of the book aside.

Put your thumb through the loop and tap the knife gently on the cushion – this will move the leaf enough for you to insert the side of the blade under it and lift it on the knife as in Fig 51; turn the knife over in your fingers and roll the leaf over so that it lies reverse side up on the front of the cushion. If it is crumpled, blow gently with pursed lips (as if saying 'who') at its centre to flatten it.

When you cut the leaf, never use scissors – they will ruin it and make a terrible mess. The correct way is to lay the edge of the knife blade on the leaf where you want to make the cut and press down firmly; push it forward a little way beyond the leaf and then draw it straight back with an even pressure and without lifting the knife until all of it is completely off the cushion (Fig 52).

When describing how to transfer the leaf from the cushion to the work, we will assume that you are right-handed; if you are left-handed you should substitute 'left' for 'right' and vice versa.

The leaf is carried on the tip; many gilders brush the tip against their cheek or hair once or twice to pick up enough natural grease to enable the leaf to cling to it. However, you will probably find it easier to put a dab of petroleum jelly (Vaseline) on the inside of your left wrist and rub it well in; if the tip is brushed lightly against this it should pick up enough grease.

Place the cushion on a table as near the work as possible and with the leaf along the front edge (Fig 53); hold the tip in your right hand and dab it down on to the front of the leaf; the movement should be quick and decisive, rather like testing something with your fingers to see if it is hot. Transfer the tip, with the leaf adhering, to your left hand between thumb and forefinger, and take up the mop with your right hand. Dip the mop into the parchment-gesso solution and moisten the area where the leaf is to go, then immediately bring the tip and leaf over the area and allow the leaf to float. Use the liner brush at the other end of the mop to disengage the leaf and to position it. Many gilders use the tip to do this and if you follow their example make sure that none of the solution gets on to the bristles, as it will soon spoil the work.

Subsequent leaves are laid to overlap each other by 3mm (⅛in), and all the overlaps should be in the same direction both horizontally and vertically. When they have all been laid the surface is 'skewed'. This is done with the tamper and consists of brushing away the excess leaf where one overlaps another; the brush must always be moved in the direction of the overlap otherwise you might lift the leaf and tear it away. Keep the skewings in a small box protected from dust etc, as they can be used for repairing small exposed faults. Such faults are dealt with by brushing and pressing down the skewings with the tamper; breathing on to the spot will help the skewings to adhere.

Before proceeding to burnishing, here are a few points to remember:

(1) When you have finished with the tip, wipe the hairs with a cotton cloth and put it between the pages of a heavy book to keep the bristles straight.

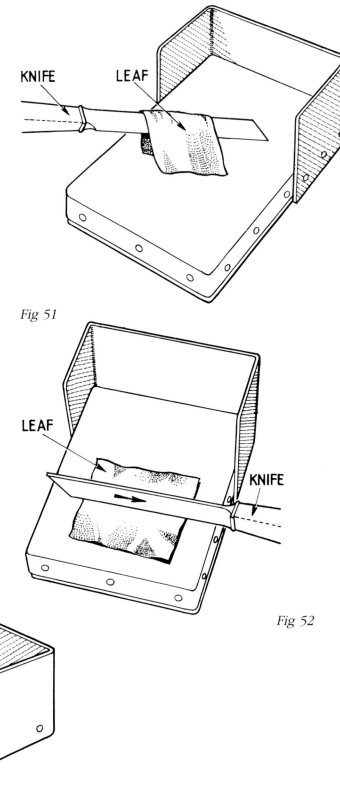

Fig 51

Fig 52

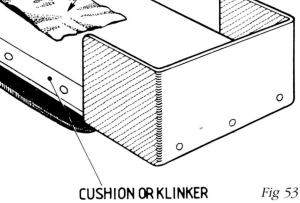

Fig 53

(2) If you do not moisten the surface sufficiently the gold will not adhere; too much gesso solution, on the other hand, will stain the leaf and make it impossible to burnish, so a little experimenting may be called for.

(3) Avoid working in draughts – someone opening the door, for instance, can blow the leaf off the cushion and you will find it very awkward to retrieve in a clean condition.

(4) Finally, it is worth rubbing some talcum powder into your fingers as it will prevent the leaf adhering to them.

Burnishing

After an hour and a half to two hours the surface should be ready to burnish. Rub the burnisher briskly with a piece of felt to warm it and then apply it to a small area; do not use much pressure at first and let the weight of the burnisher do the job. As the surface begins to become glossy, apply light pressure to the burnisher; if the surface does not respond, leave it for another quarter of an hour and try again.

Successful burnishing seems to depend to a large extent on the atmosphere, which should be reasonably damp and mild; dry, hot conditions just do not help. You should not leave the job for more than a couple of days before burnishing, but if circumstances force it to be left for longer than this, you will have to dampen the surface before starting. The best way to do this is to wet a kitchen paper towel thoroughly with water and then wring it out as dry as possible; lay a dry paper towel over the work and put the wet one on top of it and in half an hour or so the surface should be suitable for burnishing.

Continue the burnishing with a firm pressure, with the burnisher travelling in one direction only until all the area is covered; then go over it again in a different direction. A few days later, go over the burnished area yet again to accentuate the effect; only the high points are given the burnishing treatment and the contrast with the area left matt gives extra beauty. Normally the gold leaf needs no protection but if it is likely to be handled when lifting the clock, it can be given a coat of clear cellulose lacquer and this will not appreciably affect the lustre.

7 Designing your own Clock

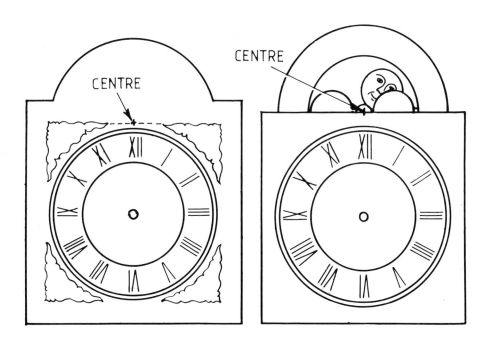

In this chapter and the next we shall be dealing with the origination of the design and construction of various clocks, assuming that you do not want slavishly to copy an existing piece, and that you are willing to use modern materials provided they do not introduce a jarring note or make your design an anachronism. As regards construction, we are sure that readers who have had experience of repairing and restoring clock cases will agree that the methods range from the highest standards of craftsmanship down to what can only be called shoddy. Therefore, we shall try to introduce standards of manufacture which follow recognised methods of cabinet making.

Let us begin with the origination of the design, using a longcase clock as a typical example. There are several ways to get ideas for your design. If you study clocks in museums or those owned by friends or relatives you can take details and dimensions. Museums are quite happy to allow this once they are assured that your intentions are serious.

Quite often, however, you have to work from photographs or illustrations in a book or magazine. Indeed, this is the rule rather than the exception with professional makers and we have often received requests for help from them when all they have to work from is a small picture cut from a magazine. There are, however, one or two ways in which you can help yourself when confronted with this problem.

If the illustration or photograph shows a front elevation (in other words, a full-frontal view) as in Fig 54, things should not be too difficult. Start by laying a piece of transparent tracing paper over the illustration and tracing off as much detail as you need. The next step is to make a paper scale. First draw a straight line alongside the traced drawing which measures the exact height; you can use this line to make the scale. Many illustrations give the height of the piece in the caption and you have to divide the scale accordingly. For instance, if the height is given as 2,285mm (7ft 6in) then the scale is divided into 90 equal parts which will give 1-inch divisions. Clearly, you will not be able to divide the line into 2,285 parts to give millimetre divisions, nor into 228 to give centimetres (unless you have superlative eyesight and a very steady hand), so it is best to work in feet and inch measurements.

Even so, the job can seem rather daunting, but fortunately there is an easy way round it as shown in Fig 55. Draw a line AC at any convenient angle to the original height-line AB, and make it of such a length that it can be divided easily into 90 equal parts, so in our example it could be 11¼in long, which can be subdivided into 90 parts, each ⅛in long. Join B to C, and then draw a series of lines

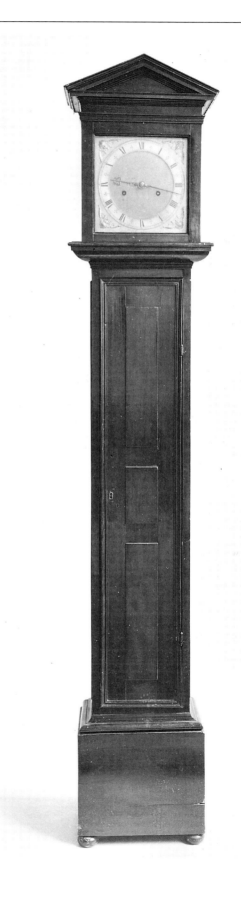

Fig 54 Longcase clock by Joseph Knibb, London c1675 (The British Museum)

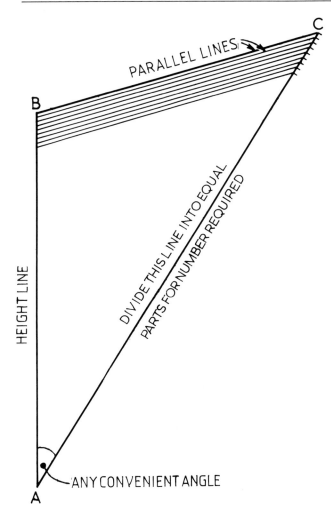

Fig 55

parallel to it; where they intersect the line AB will give you the scale. If the height is not stated on the illustration, you adopt the same method but make your scale to suit the height you want. Of course, you can make a 2in-scale by dividing the height into 45 parts, or a 3in-scale dividing by 30.

This system applies only to full-frontal views, and you can use your scale to measure not only height but width as well. However, it may be that the illustration shows the clock in photographic perspective as in Fig 54 and although you can make a scale, as described above, by subdividing the nearest vertical (as shown), you cannot use it for measuring widths. Of course, some dimensions are predetermined by the various mechanical parts – for instance, the width and length of

the trunk are governed by the arc of swing of the pendulum and the length of drop of the weights respectively; and, similarly, the sizes of the dial and the movement regulate the minimum dimensions of the hood.

This still leaves some important questions unanswered. How wide should the plinth and pedestal be? And how wide and deep is the pediment or capping? How wide is the hood overall? There is a recognised and old-established formula for determining them; it is so old-established indeed, that it was known to Pythagoras, the Ancient Greek mathematician, and it has been used ever since by architects and designers (Le Corbusier, the famous French architect, habitually used it in his work). In ancient times it was called the 'Golden Section', but from the Renaissance onwards it has been known as the 'Divine Proportion', although it is also called the 'Golden Rule', or the 'Golden Mean'.

It should be employed only as a guide and it has to be disregarded altogether when other factors have to be taken into consideration as, for instance, when designing a door frame around a square dial; obviously, the frame itself has to be square. Similarly, the measurements of a long-case trunk are determined by the length of drop of the weights in the vertical dimension and the arc of swing of the pendulum in the width.

There are other methods of deciding harmonious proportions, notably the one used by the English architect Inigo Jones (1573–1652) who appears to have been obsessed by cubic proportions. However, in our experience the Golden Rule (which is the name we personally prefer) seems to be the best for craftsmen designing in wood.

Mathematically speaking it is a visual linear expression of a geometrical progression and relates to the proportion of three magnitudes as follows: 'the first part is to the second part, as the second is to the whole or sum of the two parts'. This is mentally rather indigestible, so we have illustrated it in Fig 56A. The ratio is actually 1:1.618, which can be regarded for practical purposes as 5:8, so that a rectangle with its longer sides 8in and the shorter sides 5in gives you a

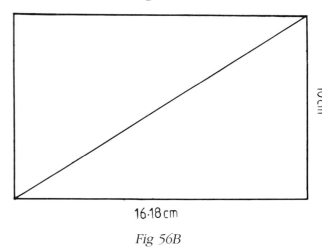

Fig 56A

Fig 56B

basis to work on. If you want greater accuracy, draw another rectangle with sides 10cm and 16.18cm, and draw a diagonal (Fig 56B): make the drawing on tracing paper and leave space to enlarge the rectangle if required. To do so, extend one of the sides to the length you want and make a mark; then draw a line at right-angles at the mark and extend the diagonal to meet it – this gives you the other side of the larger rectangle which will be in the same proportions as the original one.

Now let us apply the formula to designing longcase clock cases, with particular regard to the various kinds of hoods. First of all, decide whether you are going to make your drawing full size or to scale – if the latter, make the scale as large as possible. Next, draw a Golden Rule rectangle (we will abbreviate it to 'GR rectangle') to a suitable size for your drawing; we suggest that you use the 5:8 ratio as it is more convenient than its more accurate decimal equivalents. So it could be 40mm:64mm; or (if you are measuring in inches) 30in:48in, or any convenient size.

As we have said, the trunk of a longcase clock is predetermined but there is one other factor which governs the proportions of the remainder of the case, and that is the overall width of the waist moulding; in Fig 57A it is the line F'F. It comprises the width of the outermost circumference of the dial, plus the stiles of the door frame, plus the thickness of any side columns, plus a small allowance at each end for the projection of the waist moulding. These are all details which you have to decide for yourself but, as a guide, the door stiles average 35mm (1⅜in) wide, not including the beading; the twist columns are from 29mm (1⅛in) stock; the projection of the waist moulding, 19mm (¾in). Note that in this design the twist columns lap over the edges of the door stiles; this can be varied, of course, and there is no reason why the columns should not be free-standing as in Fig 59A, but it would make the width of the waist moulding greater.

If you study a wide range of photographs of longcase clocks you will find that in almost all cases the overall width of the base (be it a plinth, bracket feet, or turned feet) is the same as the extreme width of the hood; and the width of the waist moulding is usually about 38mm (1½in) less than those of the base and the hood. This is represented on Fig 57A by the distance X. It follows, then, that once you have established the width of the waist moulding you can easily calculate the widths of the hood and the base (Fig 57B) (E'E and R'R respectively).

Let us concentrate on the thickness of the waist moulding. It will help if you draw a vertical centre line AB and work from that. The distance AF has been established, so now draw a line from F vertically downwards, and also mark in the halfway point G. Use the GR rectangle so that its diagonal cuts the line from F at H; FH will be the proportional thickness of the waist moulding.

Now to the upper part of the hood. At the upper right-hand corner of the door frame, which is point C, position the GR rectangle as shown so that the diagonal cuts the line ER (this line is the vertical joining the extreme widths of the hood and the base) at E, thus giving you the depth of the upper hood.

The base is shown in Fig 57B. You know the width R'R as it is the same as E'E in Fig 57A and

S′S in Fig 57B. Two details which have to be decided are: first, the width of the trunk (which we have discussed already); and, second, the thickness of the bun feet. Again, you should draw a centre line and then, using the GR rectangle, plot off the two rectangles QR′S′T and QRST which give you the proportions of the pedestal.

Note that in all these illustrations such decorative details as mouldings, the pattern of bracket feet, etc, are all purely representational.

Figs 58A and 58B need little comment as they follow very closely the method used in Figs 57A and 57B. Fig 58C, however, makes the point that the centre for drawing the arch is not, as one might think, halfway between the shoulders as it is on some moon-phase dials, but centrally on a line joining the spandrels. This means that it is not a true semicircle but a segment and this should be borne in mind when drawing and working the curved mouldings on the hood which should be concentric with the arch on the dial.

The swan-neck pediment seems to have several interpretations and we show two versions, one being at a steeper angle than the other. In Fig 59A the starting point is the upper right-hand corner of the door frame, A, and the diagonal of the GR rectangle cuts the line BG at B – note that this line is the vertical projected upwards from the outside edge of the plinth. Next, build up the two rectangles BCFG and CDEF and you will find that E (and its counterpart E′) are the uppermost limits of the hood, apart from the ball and spire finial. Returning to point E, use the GR rectangle to plot the rectangle EFJK; the halfway point H between E and J is the centre for the patera or boss.

The swan-neck illustrated in Fig 59B is, in our view, a more graceful design. To draw it, start with point A (as in Fig 59A) and erect the two rectangles ABCD and BCGH – this will give you the uppermost limit of the hood, point H; draw a horizontal line through this point, and from B draw a diagonal with your GR rectangle to cut the

horizontal line at E, which (like its counterpart E′) is the top of the patera or boss. Use the GR rectangle again to plot rectangle EFKL; the halfway point, J, on the line EK is the centre for the patera or boss.

Fig 60 shows a pagoda-top hood, and the first step is to define point B. If you look at its counterpart B′, you will see that there are several factors to be decided first: whether the column is free-standing or lapped over the door frame; the diameter of the arch; and the style of the arch moulding. Having plotted these, use the GR rectangle to draw the two rectangles ABCD and CDEK. From D draw the rectangle DGFK (using the GR, of course) and mark the halfway point J between K and F. By plotting another small rectangle JKLH you will arrive at L, which is the highest point of the pagoda; F and F′ are the points where the two curves intersect. To plot the curve, join F′ to y, and then mark the halfway point Z. At Z draw a line at right angles to x, so that xZ equals F′Z or Zy; use x as the centre to draw the arc yF′.

The inverted bell hood in Fig 61 calls for the same plotting methods as a basket top and a double basket. Start at the upper right-hand corner of the door frame at point A, and put in a diagonal AB, and a longer diagonal AJ, which cuts the centre line at J. Join B to F with a horizontal line which gives you the top edge of the moulding; the line also intersects the diagonal AJ at E. From E measure off a distance along FB equal to FE which will determine point C. Next, divide EB into four parts and erect the series of six rectangles contained in ECTP; point S is the starting point of the cyma curve which runs through V to O; the two rectangles on top of each other (DCUS and SUTR) form the pedestal for the outer finial. A curve drawn from S to P will give you the shape for a basket top – a further curve drawn from P to N outlines a double basket. To continue with the inverted bell design, the finishing touch is the small capping delineated by JKMO.

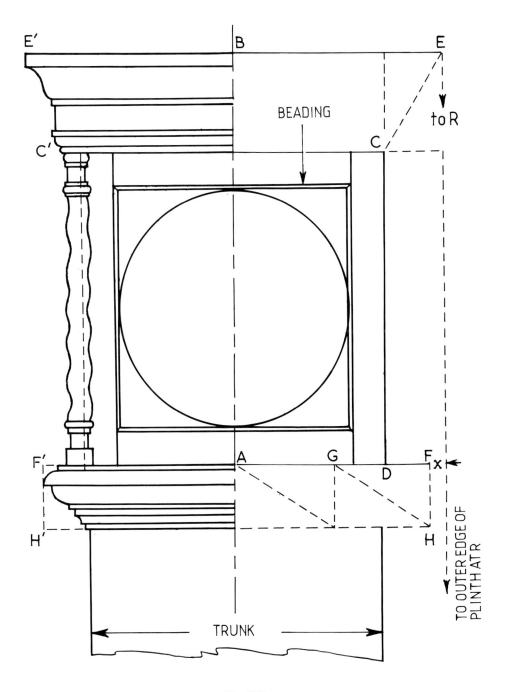

Fig 57A

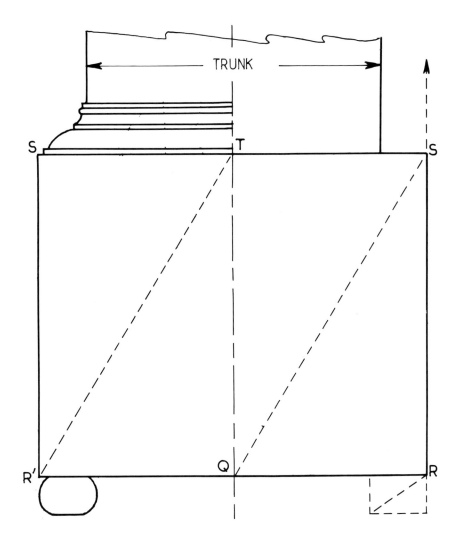

TRUNK

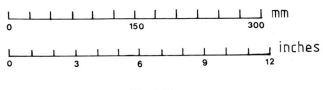

Fig 57B

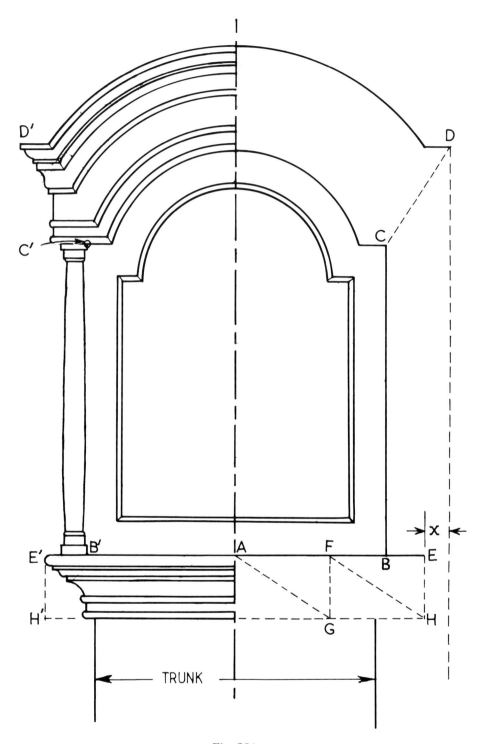

TRUNK

Fig 58A

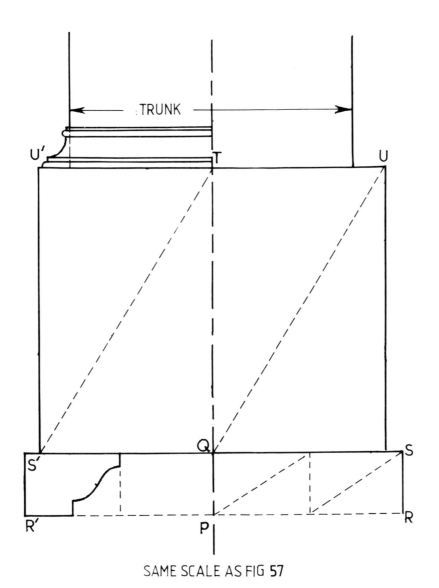

TRUNK

U′ T U

S′ Q S

R′ P R

Fig 58B

SAME SCALE AS FIG **57**

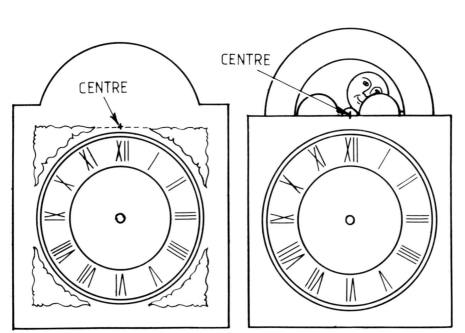

CENTRE

CENTRE

Fig 58C

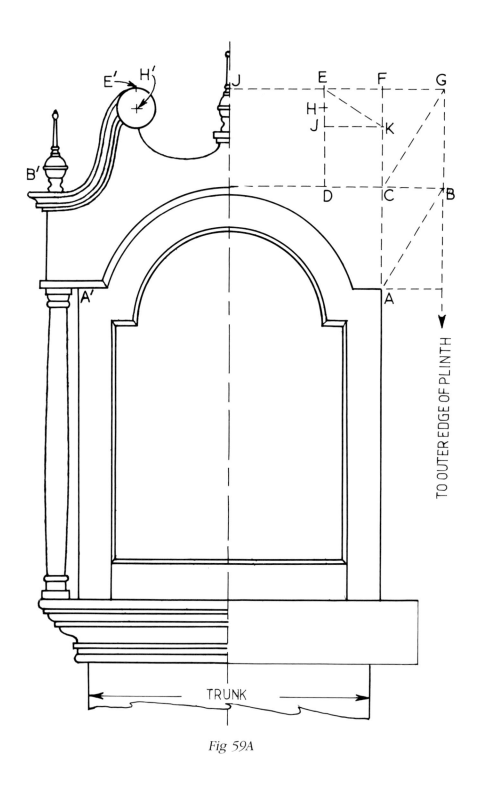

Fig 59A

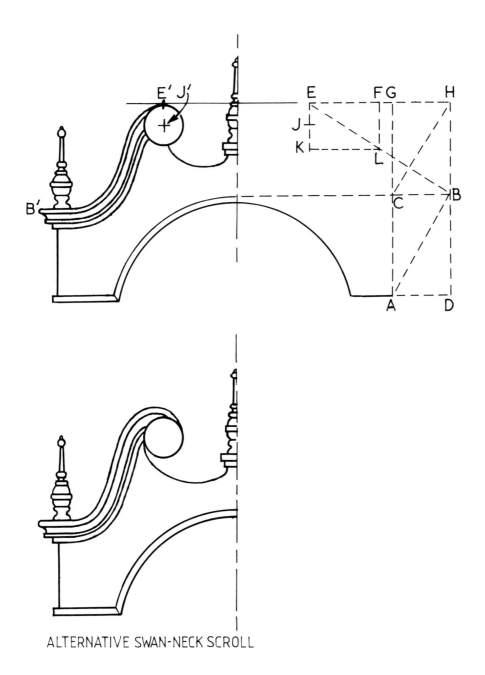

ALTERNATIVE SWAN-NECK SCROLL

SCALE AS FIG **57**

Fig 59B

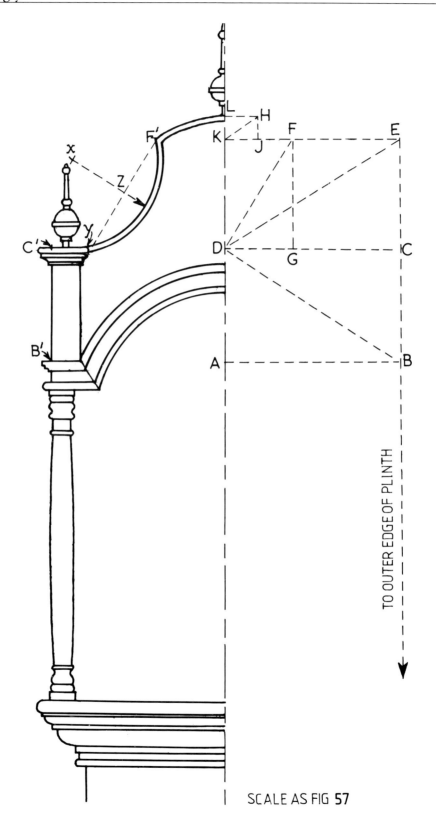

SCALE AS FIG 57

TO OUTER EDGE OF PLINTH

Fig 60

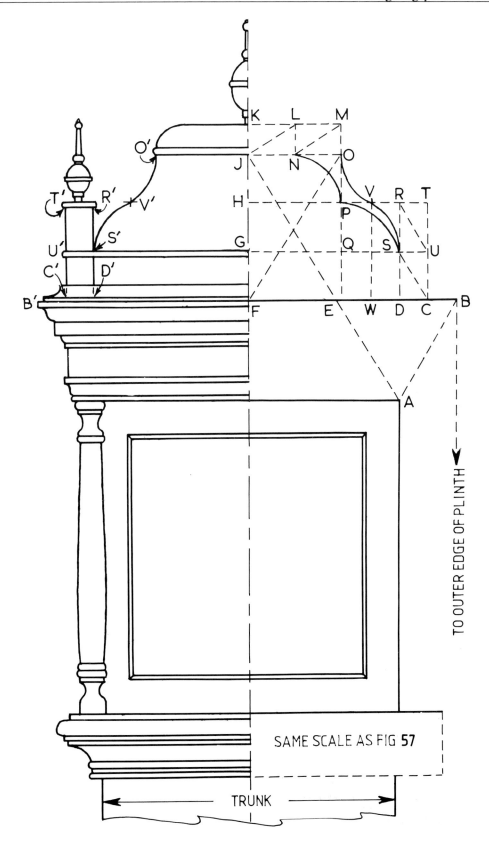

Fig 61

◇ BRACKET CLOCKS ◇

Bracket clocks (sometimes called 'table clocks') have tops or cappings which generally follow those on longcase clocks, and so the methods described above are equally applicable to both. However, there are a few extra designs which are used for bracket, but not for longcase, clocks and these are illustrated in Figs 62A–D.

The arch in Fig 62A is a lancet, or pointed arch and differs from the Gothic (Fig 62B) in the position of the centres for the intersecting arcs. With the lancet arch, you mark the halfway points on AC and BC and draw a line at right angles through each point – where these lines intersect the base line EF gives the centres for the arcs. The Gothic arch is built up around an equilateral triangle whose sides and interior angles all equal each other, so you can use A and B as centres: this arch, incidentally, can be used as the basis for a 'beehive' or 'lancet' clock top.

Fig 62C is an equilateral ogee top: the initial drawing is a square ABCD into which you inscribe the equilateral triangle ABE and the vertical bisecting line FE. By drawing a semicircle with its centre at F and its diameter AB, and then drawing arcs from C (with radius CE) and from D (radius DE) you will find they touch the semicircle at G and H respectively and give you the ogee curves.

The architectural pediment (Fig 62D) can incline at whatever angle you think looks good. The two angles (or, more correctly, pitches) which derive from classical architecture are the Grecian Doric (12½ degrees) and the Ionic (16 degrees); nevertheless, the usual tendency with clocks seems to be that a steeper pitch is better-looking, and Fromanteel's clock and most others use approximately a 28-degree angle.

Other dimensions of bracket clocks, notably the width and depth, are controlled by the sizes of the movement and dial. Figs 63 and 64 illustrate two classical designs of table clocks.

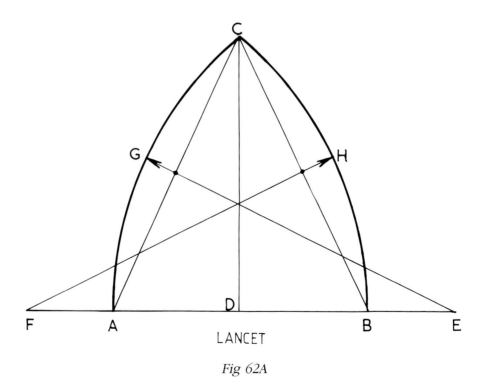

LANCET

Fig 62A

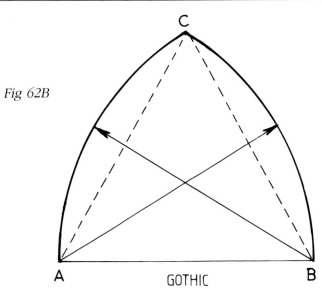

Fig 62B

GOTHIC

Fig 62C

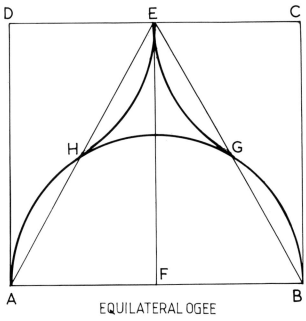

EQUILATERAL OGEE

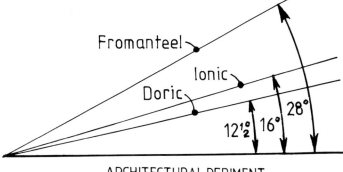

ARCHITECTURAL PEDIMENT

Fig 62D

*Fig 63 Table clock by
Joseph Knibb, London
c1695* (The British Museum)

Fig 64 Table clock by Henry Jones, London c1675 (The British Museum)

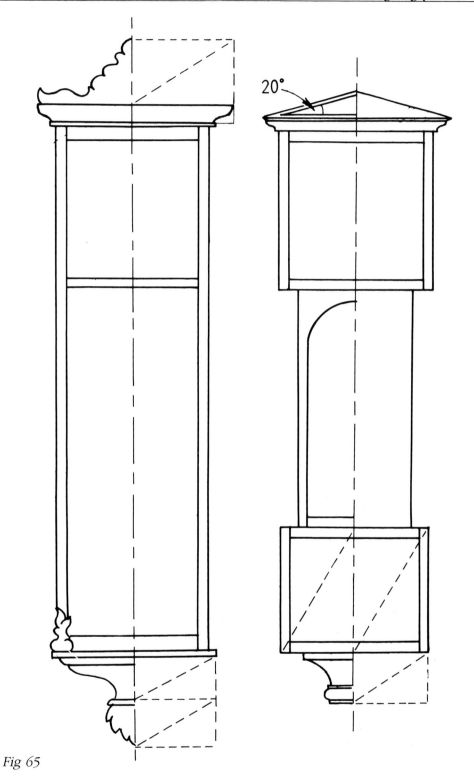

20°

Fig 65

Fig 66 Early Laterndluhr regulator. Note that the hood and the two doors are slotted into the front of the case (Gerard Campbell, Lechlade, Glos)

◇ REGULATORS ◇

Regulators were developed in the second half of the 18th century and were primarily intended to be very accurate timekeepers which could be used as controls for other clocks and watches, and little attention was paid to the decoration of the cases. This does not mean that they were indifferently constructed – in fact, the cases were invariably beautifully made and finished, but the design was plain and simple. Being purely functional, the overall dimensions were decided by the size of the movement, by the length and arc of swing of the pendulum, and by the optimum vision height of 1,422mm (56in); people were shorter at the time the clocks were introduced, and this height was the best for looking at the dial. We conclude, therefore, that the consideration of proportion in design did not apply as the design evolved from practical necessities.

Vienna regulators

Vienna regulator cases are a different matter and although the sizes of the hoods and the trunks were determined by the measurements of the dials and the pendulums respectively, the cases were adorned by a cresting of some kind at the top, and a pendant tail-piece at the bottom. Fig 65A shows how to calculate these by means of the GR rectangle and the drawing should be self-explanatory; Fig 65B illustrates a popular varia-tion and, again, the application of the GR rect-angle is evident. Note the 20-degree angle of pitch for the pediment, which appears to be the angle generally employed.

Fig 66 shows a 'Laterndluhr' regulator which is a classical design of the Vienna style.

Tavern clocks

Fig 67 depicts a shield-dial mural clock, often called a 'tavern clock'. Again, the size of the dial and the length and arc of swing of the pendulum are the two most important factors affecting the overall dimensions, but they bring with them the problem of some kind of embellishment which will make the design attractive.

Starting with a centre line, draw in the outer-most circle of the dial with its centre at Q, and follow by plotting the drop-dial casing, which is the GR rectangle EFJK. Draw in the pendant tail-piece JKLM, which comprises two GR rect-angles side by side. Now return to the line EF and draw the rectangle EFGH; the lines FC and FG are the two adjacent sides of a square CFGP which contains the ear-piece, and this is a quadrant with its centre at P. You can now plot the GR rectangle ABCD and complete the outline of the design by drawing the arch (its centre is Q) which will terminate at its points of intersection with the line AB, these points being R and S.

◇ HOODED CLOCKS ◇

Like a bracket clock, the dimensions of a hooded clock are mainly governed by the sizes of the dial and the movement; the additional ornamentation is normally some kind of simple capping, which can be designed according to the principles we have already outlined, and a 'tail-piece'. These tail-pieces vary so much in design that the only rule seems to be to make them to one's own choice, although we recommend that whatever shape is decided on should be inscribed in a GR rectangle.

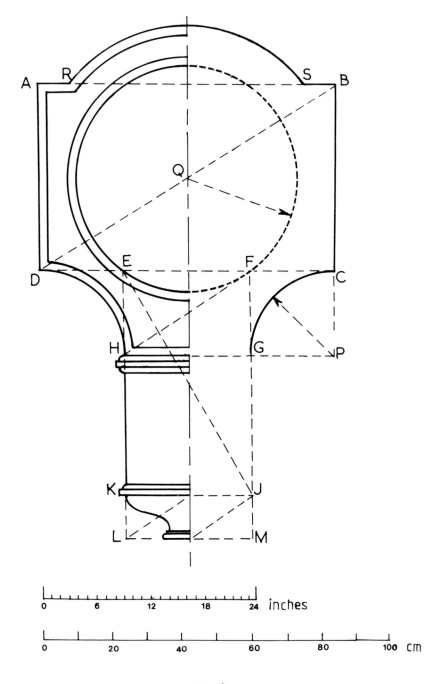

A R   S B

Q

E   F

D   C

H   G   P

K   J

L   M

0   6   12   18   24 inches

0   20   40   60   80   100 cm

Fig 67

◇ BALLOON CLOCKS ◇

A basic design for a balloon clock is illustrated in Fig 68. The first factor to be established is the diameter of the outer circle which has its centre at A; it is, of course, the diameter of the dial plus the width of the bezel and frame and this is something you must decide for yourself.

Next, we have to obtain the graceful cyma curve (often called an 'ogee' curve) and this is

quite straightforward. Draw a centre line through the centre of the outer circle, A, and then mark off two 45-degree angles as shown; this gives you the lines AB and AC whose length in each case is equal to the diameter of the outer circle. The overall width of the base, GD, is also equal to the same diameter, and the depth of the base is determined by plotting four GR rectangles side by side to develop the rectangle DEFG; it is a good idea to fix on small bracket feet which protrude slightly beyond the base. The width of the pagoda-style capping KL, is equal to the width HJ of the waist at its narrowest point, and the height of the capping is obtained by drawing a GR rectangle KLMN, as shown.

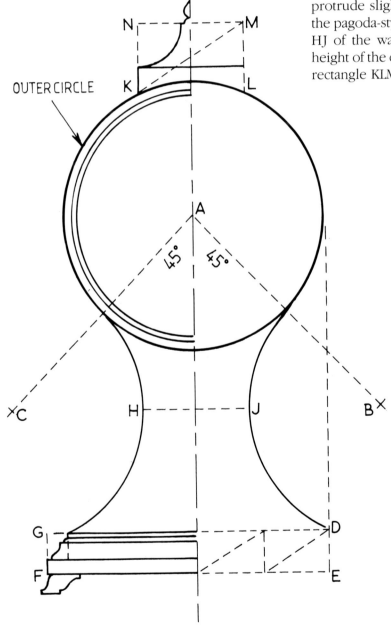

Fig 68

◇ OTHER DIMENSIONS ◇

We have dealt so far only with the front elevations of clocks, but there is also the question of the depth, front to back, to be considered. There is rarely any difficulty about calculating it, as the basic depth comprises the depth of the movement, plus the thickness of the door, plus a small clearance between the back of the movement and the inside of the case back. To this basic depth one has to add the thickness of any projecting mouldings to find the overall depth; the position of the door depends upon the clearance gap between the end of the pipe to which the hands are fixed and the inside of the glass – in longcase clocks this is usually about 12mm (½in), and slightly less for smaller clocks, say, about 6mm (¼in).

Reverting for a moment to longcase clocks, we have spent some time in studying many examples of seventeenth-, eighteenth- and early nineteenth-century clocks, in the hope of establishing some kind of representative relationship between the height of the base and pedestal as one component, and the overall height of the hood as another, the other components being the height of the trunk and the width of the waist. Despite all our endeavours we have been unable to find any standard proportions between them.

The following table may be of interest as it shows the proportions of various designs: the numbers are one-hundredths of the overall heights and are therefore percentages, eg 25 denotes one quarter. We have included one design of Chippendale's and one of Sheraton's, more out of interest than anything else as it is doubtful if either design could ever be used to house a clock.

Design	Height of hood	Height of base and pedestal	Height of trunk	Width of waist
Fromanteel: architectural pediment	22	16	62	9
Knibb: flat top, c1670	20	19	61	12½
Clowes: crested top, 1685	26	17	57	12½
Tompion: flat top, c1680	22	18	60	14
Maker unknown: pagoda top, c1720	30	21	49	15
Caddy top (USA), 1725	34	19	47	13½
Quare: bell top, c1680	30	19	51	12½
Grimes: flat top, 1695	25	19	56	13
Swan-neck (USA), 18th century	33	25	42	16
Pagoda top: George III	32	20	48	13½
Lloyd: swan-neck (George III)	33	22	45	15
MacPherson: swan-neck (George III)	30	23	47	14
Kipling: caddy top, 18th century	32	18	50	15
Ellicott: round arch, 1770	26	21	53	14½
Rimbault: round arch, 1780	28	21	51	14
Whitchurch: swan-neck	32	24	44	14
Whitman (USA): swan-neck, early 19th century	31	23	46	14
Modern British proprietary	27	25	48	17
Sheraton: arch top	31	17	52	19
Chippendale: flat top, crested	34	18	48	14

8 Making your own Clock

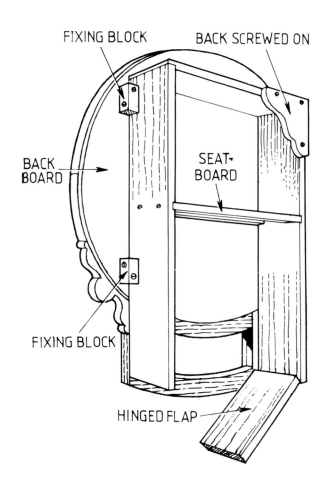

FIXING BLOCK

BACK SCREWED ON

BACK
BOARD

SEAT-
BOARD

FIXING BLOCK

HINGED FLAP

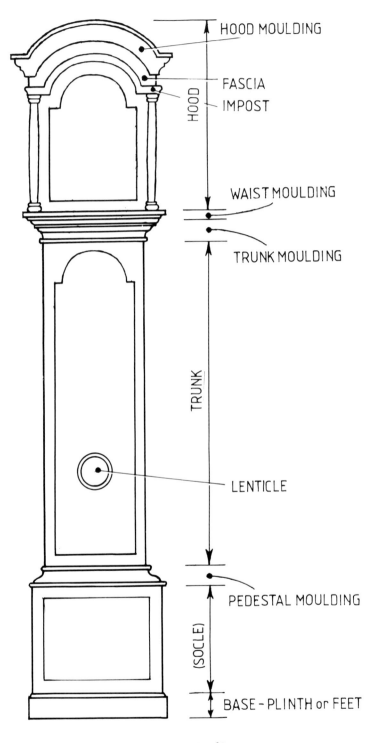

Fig 69

We now have to deal with the constructional methods employed to build various designs of clock cases. The methods we illustrate and recommend are not the only ones you can use, but they are based on good and well-tried cabinet techniques combined with those which we have seen utilised in the many clock cases we have had through our hands. To begin at the beginning, we have attempted to standardise the nomenclature of the components of a longcase clock in Fig 69. This does seem to be necessary, as different authors use different terms and this is a complication we can do without.

Most of the terms are self-explanatory; however, there are one or two which perhaps need clarification. One of these is the 'pedestal' which is sometimes called the 'base', or the 'surbase'; the correct term is 'socle', which is a plain rectangular block acting as a support for a column, but as the word is now so little used as to be pedantic, we have opted for pedestal, which is virtually the same. The other word is 'impost', which we have seen used to describe the part at the top of the trunk; however, an impost is the upper member of a pillar or column on which an arch rests and we have therefore used it to describe the spring of the hood arch.

Fig 70 illustrates a cut-away front view (A) and rear view (B) of a longcase, showing a typical method of construction; the illustration needs to be studied in conjunction with those in Fig 71.

Let us go through these illustrations, beginning with the base which can be a simple plinth, or turned bun feet, or bracket feet. Dealing with the plinth first, Fig 71B shows that it is simply a matter of fixing the plinth moulding to the pedestal front and ends (which extend to the floor) by screwing from inside, plus glue. The baseboard is glued into a trench cut in the sides and front and laps over the back bottom rail (Fig 70B) to which it can be pinned. The baseboard itself need not be more than 6mm (¼in) thick and, while it is not intended to be a strong constructional feature, it helps to keep the pedestal square while cramping up. The plinth mouldings need to be mitred together at the front corners and these can be plain butted mitres, well glued, or preferably rabbet and mitre joints as shown at

Fig 71C. Make sure that the joints are well made as they are almost always found to have opened on old (and not so old) pieces. It is well worth reinforcing the corners at the front and back with braces such as those shown in Fig 71E, screwed and glued in place. This will help to minimise any damage which could occur if the case is dragged over the floor – as happens to most clocks at one time or another.

A typical example of a bun foot is shown at Fig 71F. In the plan of the fixing details (Fig 71E) you will see that the pedestal front and ends are rabbeted and mitred together, with the base moulding pinned and glued on around the outside – this moulding is quite a small one, usually being less than 25×25mm (1×1in) in section, and provides a finishing touch around the bottom of the pedestal. It is important to glue and screw in stout corner braces into each corner as illustrated, and these must be thick enough to provide good fixings for the dowels on the bun feet. The dowels should be glued in and preferably the ends should be wedged to give a really strong fixing. Alternatively, you can dispense with the dowels and wedges and simply screw down through the corner braces into the feet, using glue as well, of course.

The method of fixing bracket feet is rather more complicated (see Fig 71G). The pedestal front and ends do not reach the floor, and the baseboard is rabbeted into the bottom edges. The bracket feet are rabbeted and mitred together at the front corners and a stout corner brace is screwed and glued in; at the back corners the bracket feet are joined together by a back bottom rail and, again, corner braces should be fixed in. The braces should be positioned so that the pedestal unit sits on them to a depth of about 12mm (½in); you will need a fillet (as shown) to conceal the bottom edges of the pedestal and also lengths of moulding which are pinned and glued in place.

Moving up to the pedestal panels, Fig 71C shows our recommended rabbet and mitre joint for the corners; although the rabbet does give extra gluing area, we suggest you use glue blocks (either merely glued or, preferably, glued and screwed) as illustrated, to give extra rigidity.

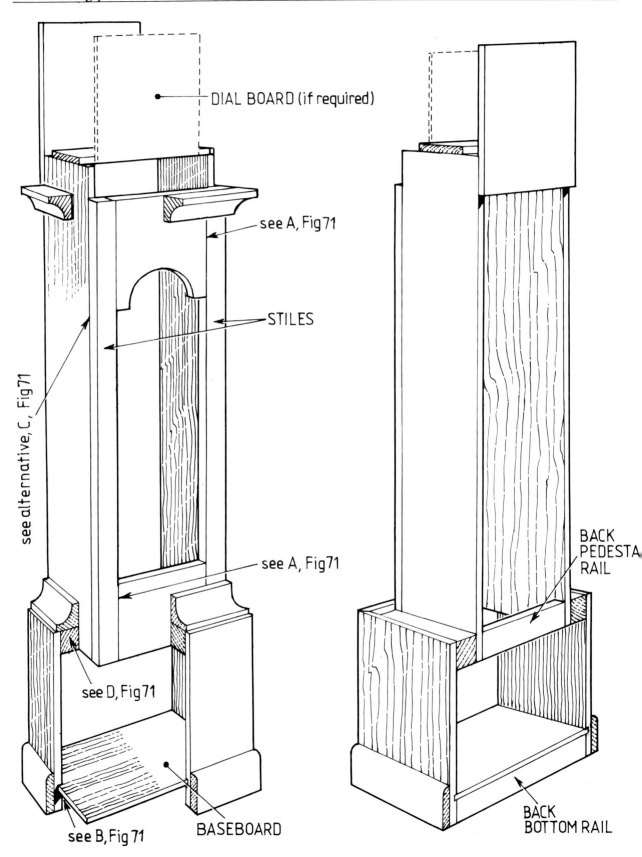

DIAL BOARD (if required)

see A, Fig 71

STILES

see alternative, C, Fig 71

see A, Fig 71

see D, Fig 71

see B, Fig 71

BASEBOARD

BACK PEDESTAL RAIL

BACK BOTTOM RAIL

Fig 70A   FRONT VIEW

REAR VIEW   *Fig 70B*

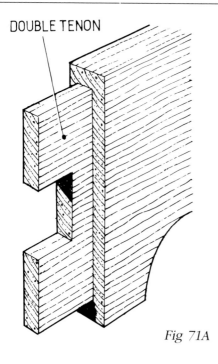

DOUBLE TENON

Fig 71A

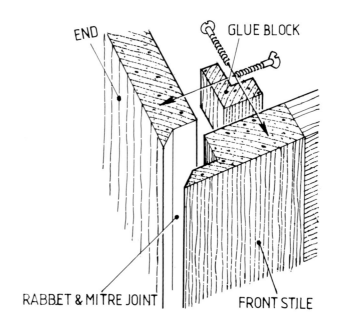

END

GLUE BLOCK

RABBET & MITRE JOINT

FRONT STILE

Fig 71C

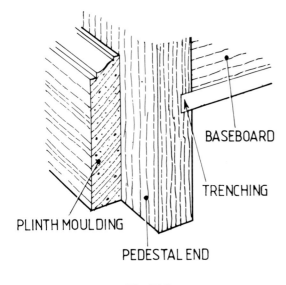

BASEBOARD

TRENCHING

PLINTH MOULDING

PEDESTAL END

Fig 71B

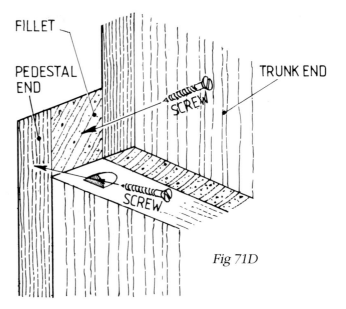

FILLET

PEDESTAL END

TRUNK END

SCREW

SCREW

Fig 71D

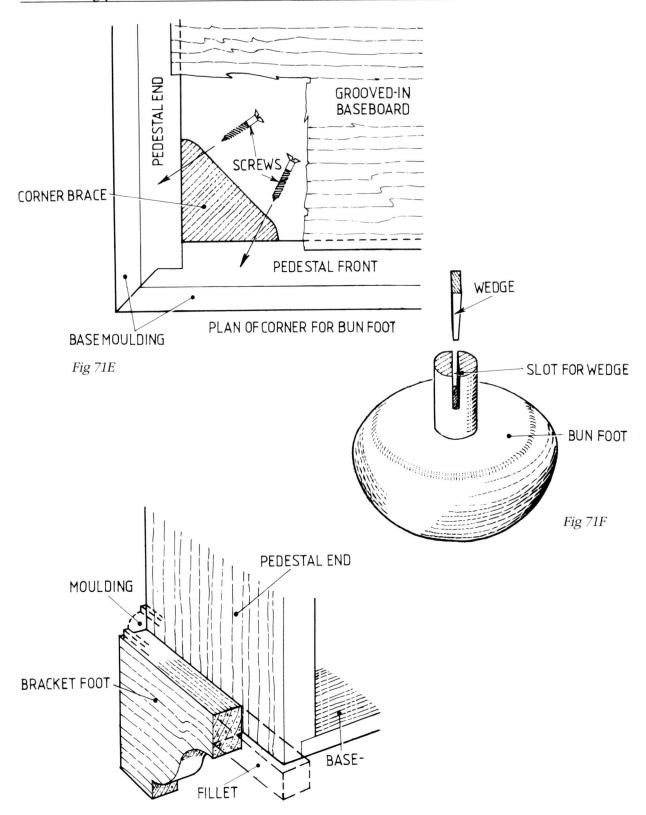

PEDESTAL END

GROOVED-IN
BASEBOARD

SCREWS

CORNER BRACE

PEDESTAL FRONT

BASE MOULDING

PLAN OF CORNER FOR BUN FOOT

Fig 71E

WEDGE

SLOT FOR WEDGE

BUN FOOT

Fig 71F

MOULDING

PEDESTAL END

BRACKET FOOT

BASE-

FILLET

Fig 71G

There is a complication at the upper end of the pedestal as the trunk is considerably narrower both in depth and width, and this necessitates the use of fillets as illustrated in Fig 71D. They can be screwed to the bottom of the trunk panels and rails, and pocket-screwed to the pedestal panels, glue being used in both cases. There is no need to mitre them at the front corners and a plain butt joint can be used as they will be covered by the pedestal moulding.

The trunk itself can be made up in either of two ways: the front can be lapped over the end panels as in Fig 70A, or the front ends can be rabbeted and mitred together like the pedestal. In the first method, the end panels have tongues worked on their front edges which mate with corresponding grooves cut in the front panel; the result is not to everyone's liking as the thickness of the front panel shows all the way down but it can, of course, be masked if veneer is laid overall. But of the two methods, we prefer the second.

The stiles and rails of the trunk are joined together with double tenons as shown in Fig 71A, and the trunk mouldings are pinned and glued in place with the front corners mitred. Don't forget that small fillets are pinned and glued on the top of each of the two side mouldings (Fig 74B) to act as guides so that the hood can be slid forwards and off. Another point to note is that the trunk sides extend upwards beyond the front and act as supports for the seat-board on which the movement (clockworks) is positioned – consequently the measurements are determined by those of the movement. Also, if you need a dial-board to fix the dial to, it can be screwed to the seat-board; obviously, it cannot in any way be fastened to the hood or the latter could not be removed. In Figs 72A–C we give three suggested designs for seat-boards; the one shown in Fig 72C is interesting as it can be adjusted for height and level.

When making the trunk door, it is a good idea to pin and glue on a lipping all round (mitred at the corners) as shown in Fig 73A. This will mean that the door laps over the aperture and will avoid the need for exact fitting; further, any movement of the wood will not be so apparent and you could, if you wish, employ a contrasting wood for the lipping.

A feature incorporated in old cases was a lenticle glass, which was a small circular piece of glass set into the trunk door at such a height that the pendulum bob could be seen oscillating behind it. It was thick blown glass and no attempt was made to polish it to obtain perfect transparency, the result being that as the bob passed the hole it was seen as a flash. Fig 73B shows how to make up the circular moulding which surrounds the hole; four small blocks of wood are glued together with the grain opposed so that as little end grain as possible is exposed. The assembled blocks can then be turned up on the lathe face-plate and sawn to the circular shape. The section in Fig 73B shows how the moulding and the glass are arranged on the door.

Another attractive development which was frequently incorporated in the trunk was the inclusion of a column inset at each front corner; a method of doing this is illustrated in Fig 73C. The trunk sides and front are sunk into the pedestal carcass as in Fig 70A, and the fillets fixed in; you will need a block (or socle) to support the column and this can be glued into the corner of the fillets and also into the strips which form the recess. If necessary, screws or pins can be driven through the strips and into the block from the inside.

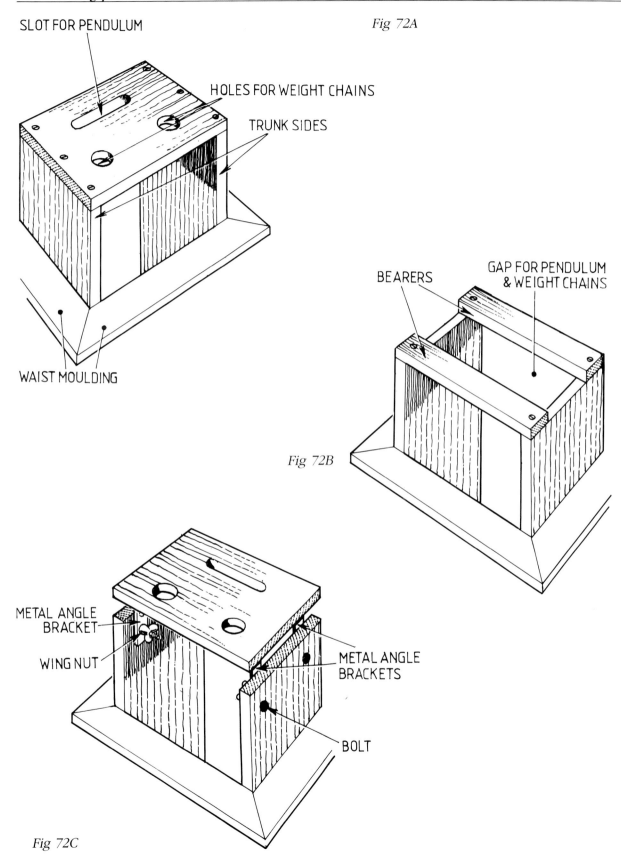

SLOT FOR PENDULUM

Fig 72A

HOLES FOR WEIGHT CHAINS

TRUNK SIDES

WAIST MOULDING

BEARERS

GAP FOR PENDULUM
& WEIGHT CHAINS

Fig 72B

METAL ANGLE
BRACKET

WING NUT

METAL ANGLE
BRACKETS

BOLT

Fig 72C

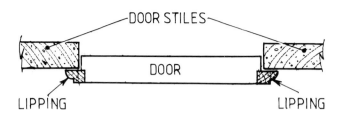

DOOR STILES

DOOR

LIPPING   LIPPING

Fig 73A

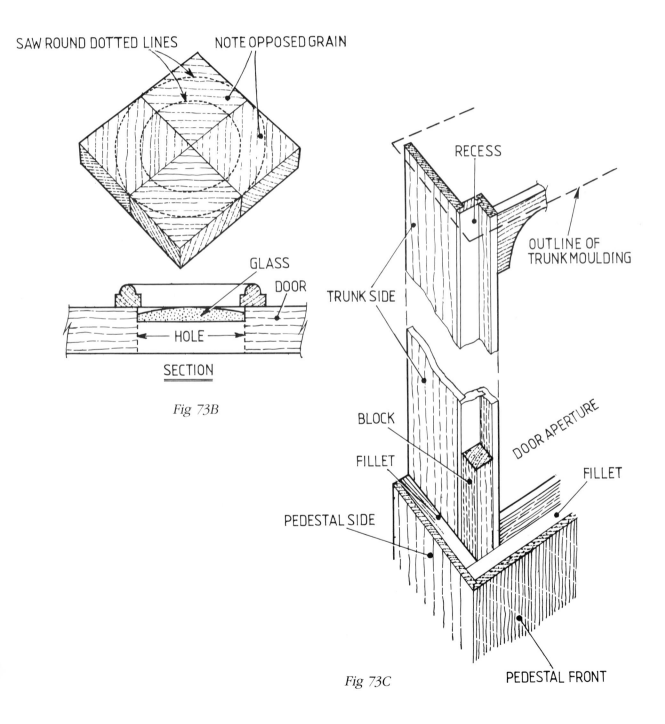

SAW ROUND DOTTED LINES   NOTE OPPOSED GRAIN

GLASS
DOOR

HOLE

SECTION

Fig 73B

RECESS

OUTLINE OF
TRUNK MOULDING

TRUNK SIDE

BLOCK

FILLET

DOOR APERTURE

FILLET

PEDESTAL SIDE

PEDESTAL FRONT

Fig 73C

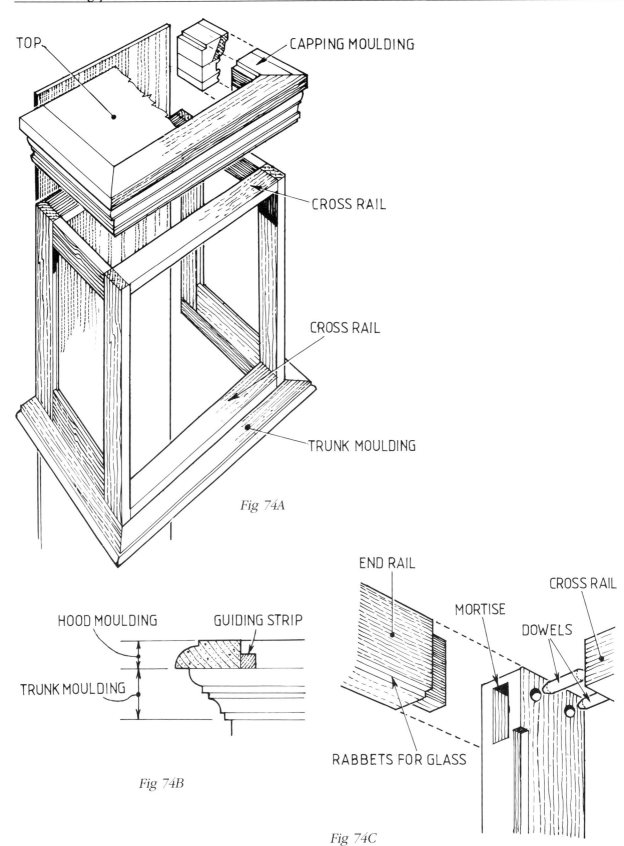

TOP

CAPPING MOULDING

CROSS RAIL

CROSS RAIL

TRUNK MOULDING

Fig 74A

HOOD MOULDING

GUIDING STRIP

TRUNK MOULDING

Fig 74B

END RAIL

MORTISE

CROSS RAIL

DOWELS

RABBETS FOR GLASS

Fig 74C

Figs 74A–C show how a simple rectangular hood with glazed sides is made up. The trunk moulding pieces are mitred together, and we recommend that the joint is strengthened with the dowels or a tongue (spline). Note that the interior faces of the ends and the trunk mouldings are flush with each other; the joint can be made with glue and dowels, or by gluing and screwing up through the trunk moulding into the underside of the end. The corner joints of the framed-up ends are conventional mortise and tenon; the cross rails are dowelled into the joints as illustrated in Fig 74C so that the dowels penetrate the tenons and lock the joint. The glass is rabbeted in all round, being held in place by a small beading, pinned but not glued on; you could groove the glass in but this would mean

inserting the glass before cramping up the frame, which could be hazardous. Further, if any of the glass should be damaged, the beading could be easily removed and a new piece of glass put in; however, if the glass is grooved in, it entails entirely dismantling the frame, which is not the easiest of jobs.

Although making up the hood door for a square dial is straightforward enough, a few complications arise when the door is for an arched dial (Fig 75A); the joints are still mortise and tenon but you have to ensure that the grain direction of the arch rail runs horizontally. Another tricky job is fitting the glass into rabbets on the inside face of the same arch rail; if the glass has the rounded arch and shoulders ready cut, then it is a comparatively simple matter to rout out the

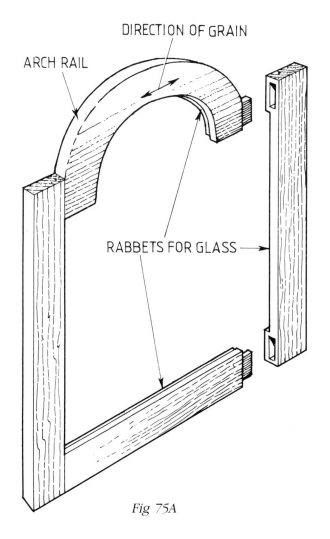

Fig 75A

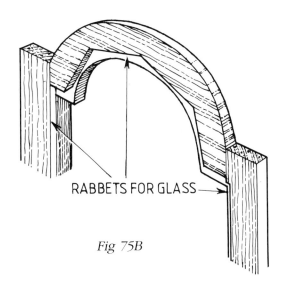

Fig 75B

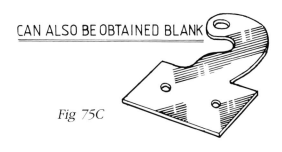

Fig 75C

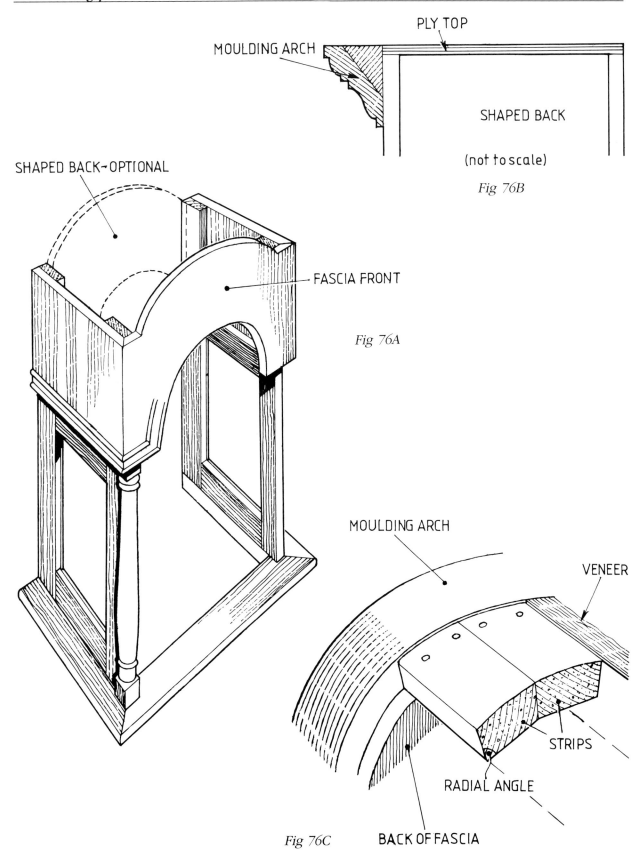

MOULDING ARCH

PLY TOP

SHAPED BACK

(not to scale)

Fig 76B

SHAPED BACK—OPTIONAL

FASCIA FRONT

Fig 76A

MOULDING ARCH

VENEER

STRIPS

RADIAL ANGLE

BACK OF FASCIA

Fig 76C

rabbet, or shape it on a spindle moulder. But if you are cutting the glass yourself and are not too confident about cutting the curve, you could adopt the method shown in Fig 75B. Here, the glass has been cut in a series of straights to conform as well as possible to the curve, and the rabbets are made to match. In both cases the glass is held in place by beadings pinned, but not glued on. This means that you need to bend the beading to fit the curve but as it is only thin you should be able to steam it to fit.

Hood doors almost always lap over the ends of the hood itself and are rarely fitted between them; this sometimes raises problems with hingeing if there are free-standing columns in front of the door which prevent it opening sufficiently. To solve this you can use a special hinge as shown in Fig 75C; such hinges can be obtained either with the screw holes already drilled, or blank, so that you can drill your own to suit.

Now we come to shaped hoods, and will deal first with the plain arched top (Fig 76A). Here, the hood stiles extend upwards and support the

fascia front and sides which are screwed to them – locate the screw holes so that they are hidden by the mouldings. The front corners can be rabbeted and mitred as already described; and the grain of the fascia should run vertically from top to bottom. Fig 76B shows a section detailing how the mouldings are glued and pinned to the fascia; if the mouldings are really heavy, they can be held by screws driven through from the back of the fascia. (All of these remarks equally apply to the swan-neck and pagoda pediments illustrated in Figs 77A and 77B; note that if you are including a finial it can be fixed to a small block glued to the fascia.)

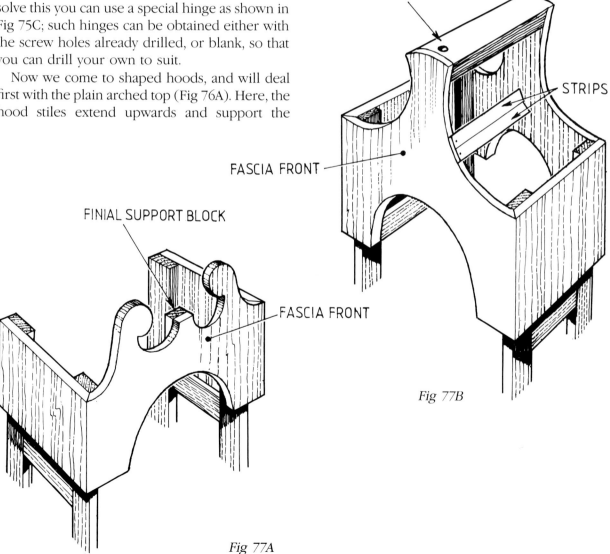

FINIAL SUPPORT BLOCK

STRIPS

FASCIA FRONT

FINIAL SUPPORT BLOCK

FASCIA FRONT

Fig 77B

Fig 77A

For the plain arch, you have the choice of: fitting a flat top which butts against the back of the fascia (this is also the type of top used with the swan-neck pediment in Fig 77A); or building a coving, curved to match the arch, which is composed of slats (Fig 76C); or using bent plywood to make the coving.

The coving does look far more elegant (although only extra-tall people can see it) but it involves more work as you have to make a fascia back shaped to match the front. The coved top itself can be thin plywood, which will probably bend easily to the curve if you have the grain running across the strip from front to back; if required, it could then be veneered. If you don't like the idea of plywood you can substitute thin strips of wood as shown in Fig 76C; these can butt up against the back of the moulding arch and be pinned and glued in place, and then veneered over. You will have to plane the edges of the strips at radial angles so that they are, in effect, coopered.

The bent plywood or coopered strips technique can be applied equally well to the pagoda pediment and Fig 77B illustrates the idea. And, although not illustrated here, the method would be just as suitable for an ogee top.

What you do about the back of a longcase is largely a matter of personal preference, as there are several ways of dealing with it. The example illustrated in Fig 70B incorporates a back pedestal rail, but this is the exception rather than the rule with old clock cases, in which the back usually ran from top to bottom. Examining the backs of old pieces of furniture is fascinating, as in some of the most imposing and elegant pieces they are reminiscent of packing cases; on the inside the backs are often covered with a silk or fabric lining to hide the imperfections. But before condemning them, one must remember that one of the most difficult problems confronting the old craftsmen was to obtain thin sheets of wood suitable for the job. There was no plywood, and all timber had to be sawn by hand; consequently, the comparatively thin wood needed for the backs would have taken hours of laborious sawing, plus more time in planing it up. Even in those days time was money, and to saw and plane up a large back would have been disproportionately expensive for a part which was rarely visible.

In our design, we recommend that you divide the back into three parts – for the hood, for the trunk, and for the pedestal – and that each back is planted on and fixed with small screws. For a really first-class job, you could rabbet the inside edges of the frames and drop panels into them, screwing the panels in. Do not use any glue, whichever method you use, as it is sometimes necessary to take off the back to do some repairs. One other point – longcase clocks were sometimes screwed to the wall to provide extra support if the floor was uneven, so if you have the same trouble do not hesitate to do the same, as there are plenty of precedents! But we suggest that instead of screwing through the back (which is, after all, not one of the stoutest parts) you fix on a cross rail at the appropriate height, screwing it to the back edges of the trunk sides, and making the wall fixing through it.

◇ REGULATOR CASES ◇

The first regulators were, as mentioned in the previous chapter, first and foremost scientific instruments and had no pretensions to being pieces of domestic furniture. Further, the cases were designed to protect the movement from damage and dust, and although they were beautiful examples of cabinet making, their appearance was strictly utilitarian.

The Laterndluhr (circa 1804) and Biedermeier (circa 1840) designs are the ones which were intended to be both elegant and useful; typical examples are shown in Figs 78 and 79 respectively. Taking the Laterndluhr first, we see that it comprises four components – hood, trunk, base and tail-piece (Fig 78A). In the earliest models, the hood was drawn forward to provide access to

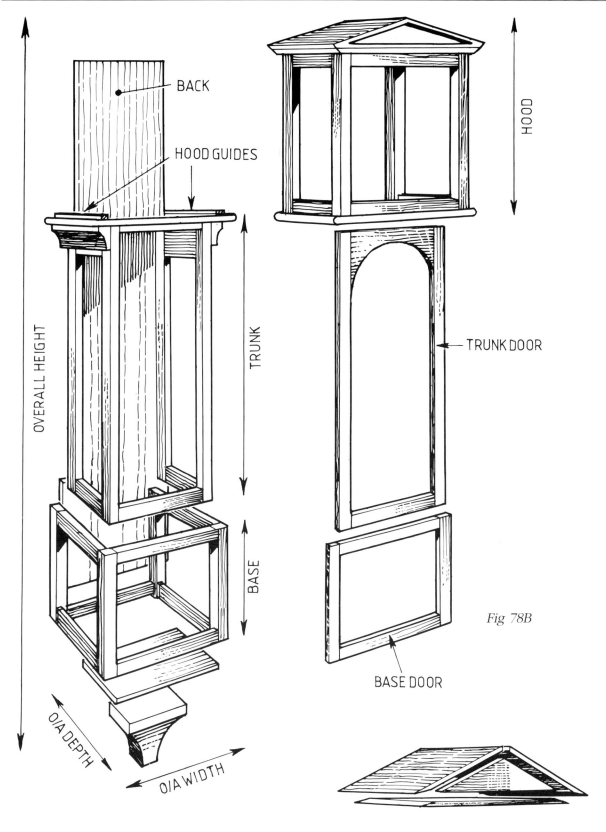

BACK

HOOD GUIDES

OVERALL HEIGHT

TRUNK

BASE

O/A DEPTH

O/A WIDTH

HOOD

TRUNK DOOR

BASE DOOR

Fig 78B

Fig 78A

Fig 78C

the movement, and two small guides were pinned and glued to the upper faces of the hood moulding, as illustrated.

Dimensions are included in the illustrations, not to be followed slavishly, but to give you a guide to the sizes of the various components. Construction is straightforward, the rails being tenoned into the stiles; Fig 78D shows the type of joint to be used where you have three members meeting. The ends of the tenons are mitred so that they meet at the junction of the mortises; this is not, strictly speaking, necessary because as an alternative you can employ short tenons which do not meet – but the mitred tenons follow the best cabinet-making tradition.

Note that the trunk assembly sits in shallow rabbets cut in the upper edges of the base and the two assemblies can be screwed and glued together. Fig 78B illustrates a complete hood which can be removed; this is preferable to having a fixed hood with a hinged door as it allows the movement to be removed more easily, if necessary. With regard to the trunk door and the base door, on early examples these simply slotted into the relevant apertures, but you will, no doubt, want to hinge them, so note that they normally lap over the ends.

Other features are the tail-piece (see Fig 78A) and the architectural pediment (Fig 78C). As it is comparatively small, the tail-piece can be cut from the solid, using two pieces glued together if

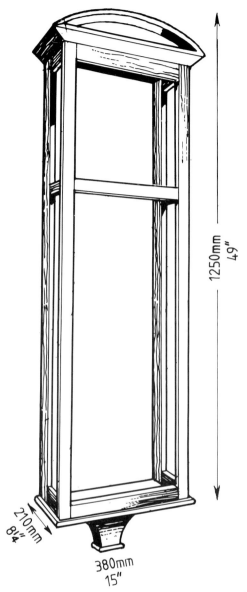

Fig 79

needed. The main problem with the pediment is that of bevelling the edges to form the mitres, and these bevels can be sawn or planed roughly to the angles required, the final smoothing being achieved with a sander.

The Biedermeier design (Fig 79) requires little comment as the constructional methods have already been fully explained. The style usually called for elaborately carved crestings, brackets and tail-pieces, and if you are not too confident about your carving abilities, you will have to buy them in.

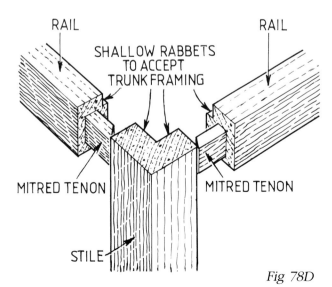

Fig 78D

◇ BRACKET CLOCK CASES ◇

Fig 80 illustrates a typical bracket clock; dimensions are again given, but you will have to adapt them to your personal requirements. All constructional features have been dealt with earlier in this chapter; there are several points to note, however:

1 The door normally laps over the ends with a lock on the left-hand stile.

2 The seat-board is a small block pinned and glued to the bottom of the case.

3 It is worth rabbeting the door at the back into the edges of the case to exclude dust. This door can be either arched to match the one at the front, or a plain rectangle.

4 The front door can either be made to lock, or have a simple hook and eye.

5 If the door is crossbanded, it is rare to find a mitred joint at the corners.

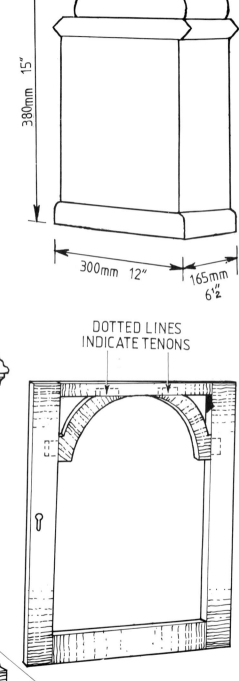

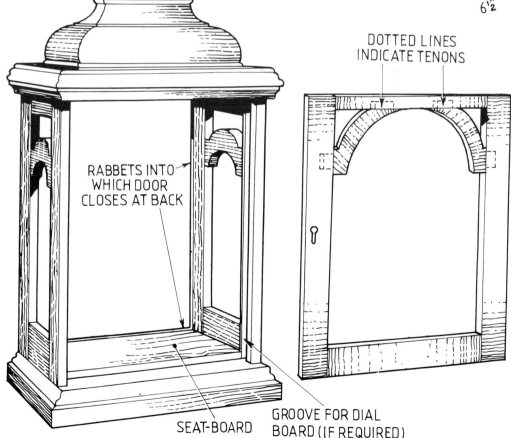

Fig 80

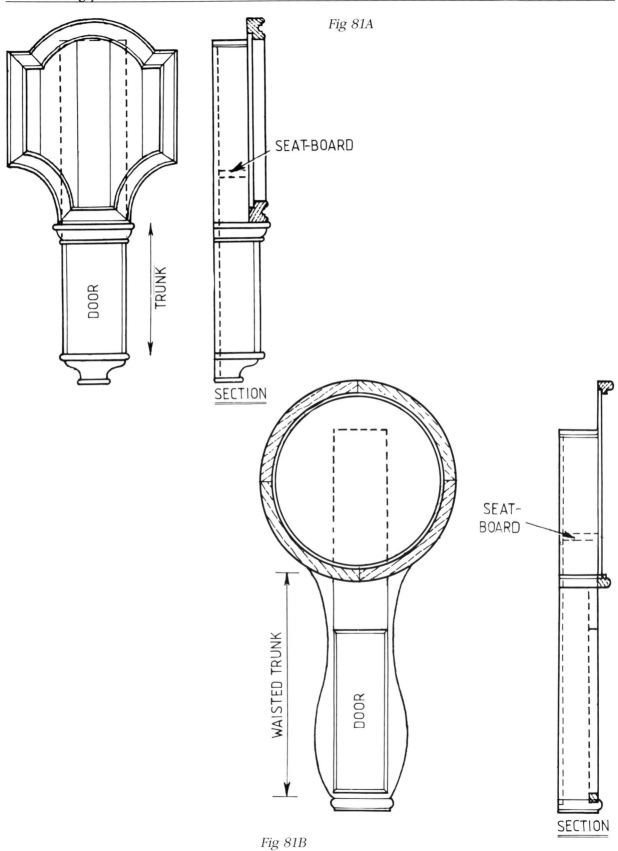

Fig 81A

SEAT-BOARD

DOOR

TRUNK

SECTION

SEAT-BOARD

WAISTED TRUNK

DOOR

SECTION

Fig 81B

◇ TAVERN OR MURAL CLOCK CASES ◇

Fig 81A shows a shield style, drop-dial clock; and Fig 81B a circular drop-dial clock. Both designs appeared circa 1735 and were painted or japanned, and the dials were composed of boards, tongued and grooved together. The sizes of the dials varied enormously – from 380mm (15in) to 760mm (30in) in diameter, and consequently they were unglazed; by about 1790, however, the dials became smaller and the painted or japanned decoration gave way to polished wood.

Tongued and grooved boards are liable to move with fluctuations of humidity in the atmosphere and the result can often be seen in old examples, where the boards have come slightly apart and split the paint or japan coating. If you want to use this form of construction in the interests of authenticity, then make sure that the timber has been seasoned to the correct moisture content (10 to 14 per cent). The best way to do this is to store it indoors in an atmosphere with this moisture content, which is the one that prevails in the average house.

Machine the tongues so that when the boards are cramped together they do not reach the bottom of the grooves; if they do, and subsequently swell, the whole dial will buckle. Also, match the boards side by side with the heart sides alternating so that the effect of 'cupping' (ie, twisting) is minimised (see Fig 81C). Do not glue the boards together but allow the mouldings to contain them; as you can see from the sections, the boards lie in a rabbet on the back of the mouldings.

It follows that the mouldings have to be firmly fixed together at the mitres and the best way to do this is by inserting dovetail keys (Fig 81D) on

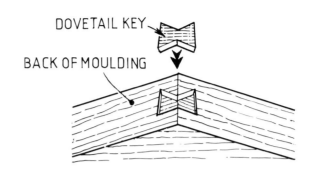

Fig 81D

the backs of the mouldings. In the case of the circular bezel illustrated at Fig 81B, the four segments which comprise it are mortised and tenoned together and this should make a strong frame.

The cases behind the dials have to be robustly constructed as the falling weights are very heavy. Our suggestions are shown in Figs 81E–G: the bottom corners have shallow rabbets and the parts are glued and screwed together; the side rails of the seat-board are also located in a shallow trench and then screwed and glued. The back can be simply screwed on to the carcase, while the top can be pinned and glued, or glue-blocked as it does not need to be strong but merely keeps out dust.

One method of constructing the waist feature of the circular drop-dial clock is shown in Fig 81F, where the swell pieces are deep-sawn and dowelled to the case sides, and then veneered; two or even three pieces can be glued together if necessary to make up the requisite thickness. A different way to create the waist is shown at Fig 81G, where a single thickness is sawn to shape and dowelled to the case side.

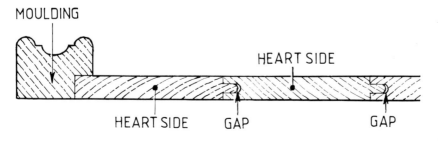

Fig 81C

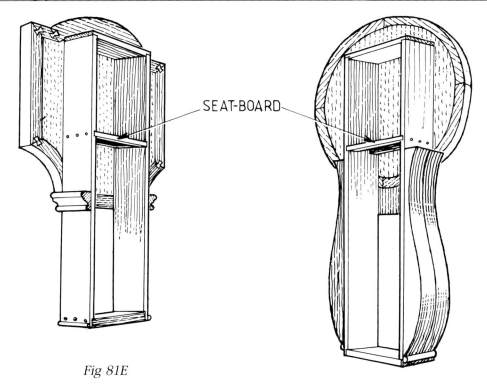

SEAT-BOARD

Fig 81E

Fig 81F

As mentioned, it is impossible to show sizes as the dials vary so much in width, and the length of the case is determined by the length of fall of the weights. This is further complicated by the fact that it was discovered that to provide an eight-day duration of going, the weights had to fall an unacceptable distance. To solve this problem, a fifth extra wheel was added to the movement and this was combined with a heavier weight. What we can definitely stipulate is that all parts should be sufficiently thick, and we would recommend that they are worked out of 25mm (1in) stock.

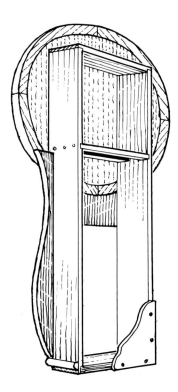

Fig 81G

◇ WALL CLOCK CASE ◇

This is the clock which is familiar to most of us as it was (and is) used in schools, public buildings and similar places. As it is spring-wound, the case need not be very strong as it only serves to house the movement and pendulum (see Fig 82).

The circular frame is made up from segments mortised and tenoned together as already described; an additional feature is the rabbet worked on the front inner edge which accepts the glass, and a metal bezel is fixed over this. A backboard is pinned and glued to the back of the frame, and this needs to be drilled for the pipe and for winding; the case is held to the frame by means of four fixing blocks screwed and glued in place (Fig 82C).

As we have said, the case does not need to be robust and 9mm (⅜in) stock should be suf-ficiently thick. The case top is rabbeted over the ends and the joint glued and screwed; the seat-board is housed into the ends and also glued and screwed in place, and these two cross-members serve to keep the case square. Note the hinged flap which gives access to the pendulum; it is held in place when closed with a simple hook and eye.

When you come to draw out the shape of the curved, glazed panel under the circular frame you can see that the curves are concentric with it; you must be sure to make the width of the bottom rail wide enough to conceal the hinged flap (see dotted lines, Fig 82A). Fix the glass in as shown in Fig 82B. The ear-pieces can be either pinned or dowelled, and glued to the frame, and the back can be simply screwed on.

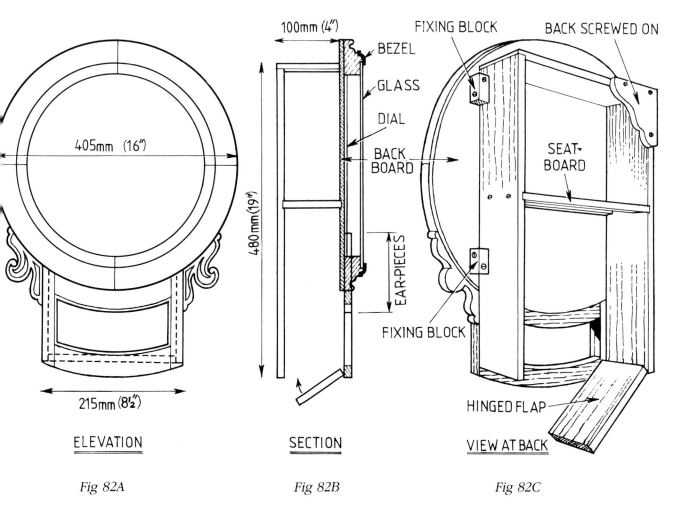

ELEVATION

Fig 82A

SECTION

Fig 82B

VIEW AT BACK

Fig 82C

◇ HOODED WALL CLOCK ◇

This is shown in Fig 83; the construction is straightforward, and as all joints, etc, are as described earlier, there is no need for further explanation. The case needs to be fairly strong and we recommend 16mm (⅝in) stock; if a dial-board is required it can be fixed to the front of the seat-board.

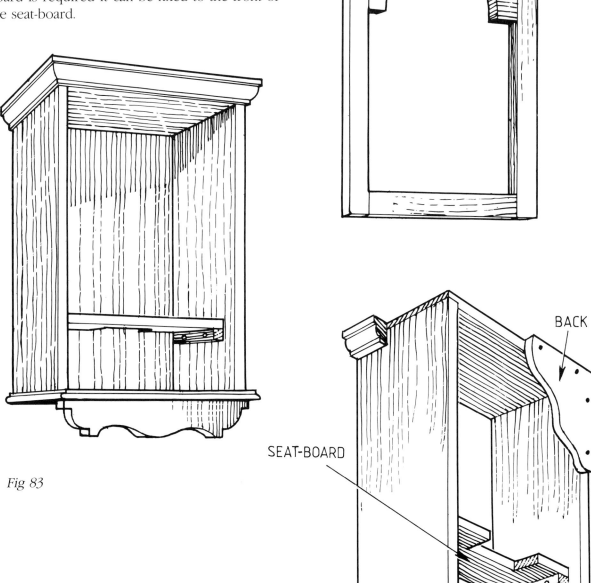

Fig 83

BACK

SEAT-BOARD

HOLE FOR PENDULUM & WEIGHT CHAINS

◇ BALLOON CLOCK ◇

This attractive clock, illustrated in Fig 84, happened to come into the workshop for extensive restoration, and it is a good specimen of the type. It is made of beech cut by hand from solid pieces (Fig 85); the two side-members are deep-sawn and pierced for glass panels mounted in rabbets on the inner surfaces. It can be seen that the top and bottom members are inserted into dovetail slots and fox-wedged in, thus avoiding the use of metal fixings of any kind. All the metal is hand-made including the screws used for fixing the door catch and movement, and the hook and ring hinges for both doors.

The bracket and top (Fig 86) are both made from two solid pieces to make the waste removal from the back a much simpler operation – this being done with saw and chisel with no attempt to achieve a good finish. The small capping is glued on and the wooden spheres are attached with small dowels. The small bead is worked in the solid on both smaller sections, not applied after.

Fig 84

As a matter of interest the dimensions are as follows:

Height of clock with top	640mm (25¼in)
Width at feet	360mm (14¼in)
Depth	120mm (4¾in)
Bracket height	200mm (8in)
Bracket width	360mm (14¼in)

The door to the front is a very delicate bit of work, the whole thing being again of beech; and the back is rabbeted to fit into the carcase. The top is bevelled on the inner surface to receive the convex glass for the dial and rabbeted to take the lower glass which allows the pendulum to be seen. The original finish was dark green paint with gilt finish to the front door, the feet, the beads on the bracket and the top as well as the cappings and spheres.

Fig 85

Fig 86

9 Decorative Veneering

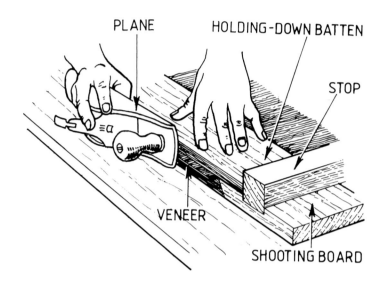

PLANE

HOLDING-DOWN BATTEN

STOP

VENEER

SHOOTING BOARD

◇ CROSS-VENEERING ◇

This term refers to the veneering of narrow strips where the grain runs crosswise, for example on a glazed door. It differs from *crossbanding*, which is always a border to a panel, table-top, or the like. Crossbanding is, however, laid in a very similar way and the method described here will serve for both. So you should get a good idea of the work involved.

Dealing first with a door which has no panel and is simply an open frame, you must decide whether the edges are to be veneered. If so, this job must be completed before the faces are veneered. Remember to check that the door will still fit after the edge veneers have been applied.

All surfaces to be veneered first have to be toothed (this applies to flat panels, too). This is best done with a toothing plane, which has a series of serrations cut along the length of the cutting iron so that whenever it is sharpened, the cutting edge presents a row of teeth across its width. The cutting iron is held almost vertical in the body of the plane so that it will cut a series of grooves which afford a good key for any glue and smooth out any irregularities. If possible it is worked in all directions, but in the case of narrow strips you will have to take it along the lengths of the rails and stiles.

However, it is not essential to use a toothing plane, and you can substitute a piece of really rough glasspaper wrapped around a glasspapering block. You must ensure that the glasspaper is kept absolutely flat on the work so that you do not dub or round off the edges. Or you could use a rasp, and again you must guard against dubbing over the edges.

Before cutting your piece of veneer into strips, trim the edge off it as shown in Fig 87A. Here, the veneer is laid on a shooting-board and allowed to project slightly over the edge, and a piece of batten is pressed down as near the edge as possible to prevent buckling. The smoothing plane needs to be set very fine so that the chances of splitting the veneer are minimised.

It is a good idea to draw a line lightly with a piece of chalk right across the show-face of the veneer; this can be removed later with a damp

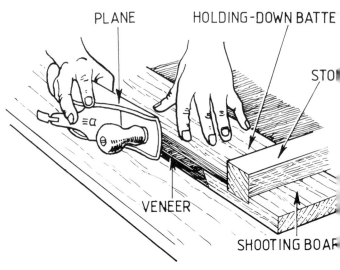

Fig 87A

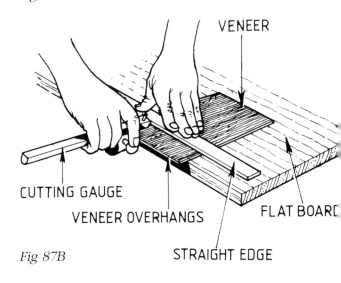

Fig 87B

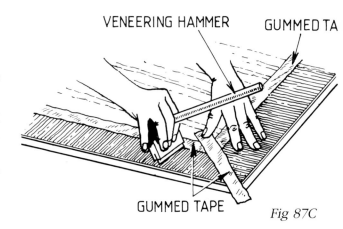

Fig 87C

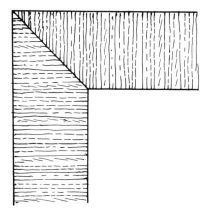

Fig 88A

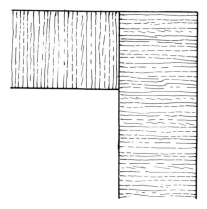

Fig 88B

Both the hammer and caul methods of laying veneer are described later in this chapter; Fig 87C shows an alternative way of holding the hammer. (Note, too, the gummed paper tape which should be stuck down as you progress.)

If the frame you are cross-veneering has a 'stuck' moulding on the inside edges (ie a moulding worked in the solid), the best way is to cross-veneer the frame first, then cut through the veneer with a cutting gauge and, finally, work the moulding (Fig 89).

VENEERED RIGHT TO EDGE

GAUGED CUT IN VENEER

FINISHED JOB

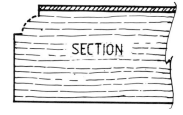

Fig 89

rag. The chalk line will ensure that you always lay the same surface uppermost; this is important, as if you lay it with opposite faces showing you are likely to get an unacceptable variation of shading.

The next task is to cut off the strips, and the recognised way of doing this is shown in Fig 87B, using a cutting gauge. You can, of course, use a sharp veneer or craft knife; in any event, you need a perfectly flat board to lay the veneer on with its edge overhanging, and a straight edge to guide your gauge or knife. There is no need to trim each strip after it has been cut as it will have to be trimmed after laying; obviously, you need to allow a bit extra for this when measuring the width of the strip. Now is the time, however, to cut and trim the corner joints to be mitred (Fig 88A), or butted (Fig 88B), and this can be done on the shooting-board, as already described.

◇ LAYING HALVED AND QUARTERED VENEERS ◇

The difference between halved and quartered veneers is illustrated in Fig 90. In a halved and matched panel, two consecutive leaves of veneer must be used so that the result is a mirror-image of the two halves; similarly, four consecutive leaves have to be used for a quartered panel. Such panels can be cramped up in a caul press (as described under Oyster Veneers, on page 134) or laid by hammer. The latter method is preferable as veneers can stretch or buckle when cramped up and this can play havoc with the joints. The method described below is best undertaken with Scotch glue.

When hammer-veneering, you should leave an overlap of about 25mm (1in) on the meeting edges of the pieces (Fig 91). For halved panels, lay one of the leaves first and press down with the hammer (Fig 92A). Next, lay the matching half with its overlap coinciding with that of the first, and lay a straight edge along the centre line, holding it firm with a couple of small cramps if you wish. Cut through both thicknesses of veneer with a veneer knife (or a craft knife) with a single cut (Fig 92B). You can remove the overlaps as waste, taking off the top one first and then lifting the edge of the veneer to pull away the bottom overlap (Fig 92C). Quartered veneers are laid in the same way, two adjoining pieces being laid first. Sticking lengths of gummed paper strips over the joints in both cases will help to keep them butted together as the glue dries out, and the safest and most convenient way to hold the panels in place is to cramp them between cauls until the glue sets finally.

If you are jointing curl veneers, it is advisable to shoot the edges a trifle hollow at the centre because curls have a nasty habit of swelling out at the centre when dampened, causing the ends of the joint to open. The veneer may buckle when you tape the joint and force the centres together but it will flatten out easily when in the caul.

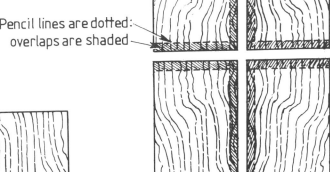

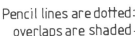
Pencil lines are dotted; overlaps are shaded

Fig 91

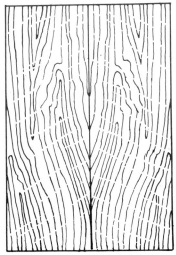

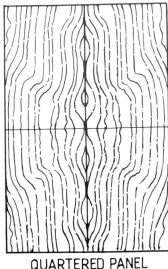

HALVED PANEL   QUARTERED PANEL   *Fig 90*

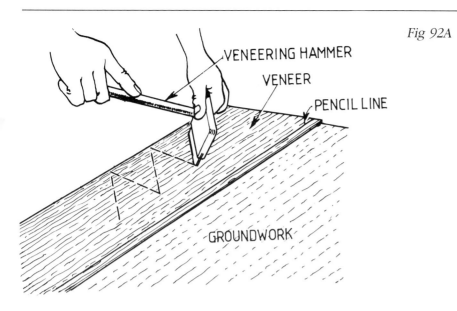

Fig 92A

VENEERING HAMMER

VENEER

PENCIL LINE

GROUNDWORK

Fig 92B

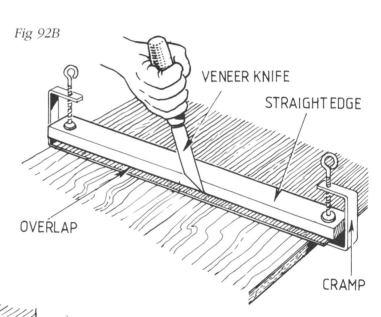

VENEER KNIFE

STRAIGHT EDGE

OVERLAP

CRAMP

Fig 92C

LOWER WASTE STRIP

◇ OYSTER VENEERS ◇

Properly laid, these can give a most beautiful effect which transforms an otherwise ordinary piece into something of elegance. But be warned – the whole process is very time-consuming and can be fraught with difficulties, most of which seem to occur in the later stages when you think things are going well.

Oysters are thin slices cut transversely across a log; if they are cut at right angles the result is a roughly circular oyster, but often the cut is made at an angle of about 45 degrees which yields an elliptical shape. Several different woods can be converted in this way, among them laburnum, yew, olive, mulberry, kingwood, and walnut.

Undoubtedly the single most important factor is the seasoning of the log. The ideal log should be as straight as possible and free from knots and splits; it should be of as small a diameter as possible while being adequate for the sizes of oysters required. Do not use an old log which has been lying around for several years, as quite often the sapwood may have become soft and/or discoloured. The best choice is a log which has been cut and left to dry for six to twelve months, with the cut ends sealed with a coat of paint or paraffin wax.

Sawing the oysters is the next consideration, and for cuts at right angles to the length you can use either a bandsaw or a sawbench. If you do the job on a bandsaw, use the widest saw blade possible to minimise deflection and vibration – in practice this means a 19mm (¾in) blade as a minimum. For cuts across the log at an angle other than a right angle it is easier to employ a sawbench. And, of course, safety is something which has to be borne in mind; if the design of the finished oysters allows it, plane off a flat along the log so that you can rest it safely on the saw table. The alternative is to make a cradle as shown in Fig 93 into which the log can be cramped.

The thickness of the oysters must be as consistent throughout as possible, because when they are laid they have to be sanded to a uniform thickness: if they are to be inset into a veneered surround on an old clock case which has saw-cut veneers, this can well be about 3mm (⅛in). A point to note is that the sawdust should be swept away after each cut, otherwise the ensuing cut will be narrower than it should be. You should be prepared to lose almost as much wood making sawdust as making oysters.

The trickiest part of the whole operation is the final seasoning of the cut oysters prior to laying. The problems are really those of controlling the release of tensions due to the oyster no longer being part of the log, plus drying out any residual moisture, and both these factors can cause distortion. Unfortunately this is what happens in most cases, and you must realise that the failure rate can be up to 50 per cent.

In the old days the craftsmen stored the oysters upright in a box containing fine sawdust. The purpose was to equalise the moisture content of the oysters with that of the surrounding atmosphere slowly and gently to prevent undue stress on the grain, and the sawdust acted as an equaliser. This process, of course, did nothing to keep the oysters flat and allowed them to buckle freely. This was an advantage as it meant that when the oysters dried out there was no further movement – one must bear in mind that room temperatures in those days were much lower than in these days of central heating, and the humidity was correspondingly higher.

The next stage was to flatten the oysters and they did this by dampening them slightly with a thin solution of glue size and water, and placing them between a pair of boards with a medium weight on top. A number of oysters could be flattened in this way, with thin sheets of wood being sandwiched between the veneers. Usually a day was long enough for this to bring results, and the oysters were then laid with Scotch glue.

This method is the one we have always used and it is the only one suitable for restoration work or for a reversible bond, but we must emphasise that to ensure compatibility Scotch glue must be used for laying oysters when glue size has been employed. We have updated the way in which pressure is applied, by using cauls and cramps as shown in Fig 94 and we interleave with sheets of blotting paper instead of sheets of wood. Note that the cauls are slightly convex, ie thicker in the centre than at the edges. This is important because it ensures that as the cauls are cramped together, any moisture is driven to the outside where it can disperse easily; if the cauls are flat, the moisture is driven further into the oysters and takes much longer to dry out. If you warm the cauls before use (but do not make them too hot to handle) it will expedite the process.

An alternative method is recommended by Mr David Withers, an expert who used it during his time as a student in furniture restoration at the London College of Furniture; a description is given in *Woodworker* magazine, November 1981. He found that if oysters were immersed in PEG (polyethylene glycol 1000) and then put between sheets of thick cartridge paper under weights and left for one to four months (depending on the size of the original log, its moisture content, and the thickness of the oysters) the results were good. However, he pointed out that oysters treated in this way must not be glued down with any adhesive either containing water or needing heat, so Scotch glue would have to be replaced by a modern PVA adhesive.

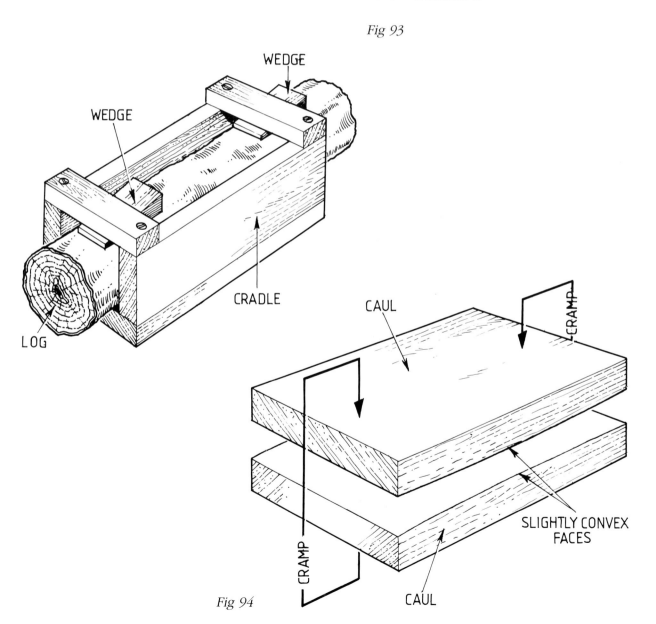

Fig 93

WEDGE

WEDGE

CRADLE

LOG

CAUL

CRAMP

CRAMP

CAUL

SLIGHTLY CONVEX FACES

Fig 94

◇ VENEERING SHAPED WORK ◇

It is inevitable that this problem will arise sooner or later and whatever methods are used to overcome it, you will have to be resigned to an occasional failure. All you can do is to take all precautions possible and scrupulously follow the correct sequence of operations. The clock bracket illustrated in Fig 95 exemplifies most of the technical points involved. We have divided it into two parts: the convex curve at A, and the concave coving at B.

If you are making a clock for yourself it is permissible to use a contact adhesive which is non-reversible (ie which cannot be softened or removed without damage to the veneer and groundwork); it certainly makes the job much easier as there is an instant bond between the two coated parts and consequently no need for cramping.

For all other adhesives, including our favourite Scotch glue, you have to devise some means of holding the veneer to the groundwork while the adhesive sets. But there are a couple of general points which apply, whatever adhesive is employed.

The first is that it is a good idea to dampen the veneer and position it on the groundwork, without adhesive, so that it takes up an approximate curve. It can be held in place with rubber bands and left overnight; but remember that the veneer must be allowed to dry out thoroughly before any adhesive, except Scotch glue, is applied.

The second point is that unless each component part of each unit A and B is veneered first and then assembled, there could be gaps between the edges of the veneers at the arrises (the meeting edges). The procedure is shown in Fig 96; the parts of the groundwork are shaped and dry-assembled first to check their correctness, then dismantled and veneered. The veneers are allowed to lap over the edges on each part, and once the adhesive has set the overlaps are trimmed flush and the parts finally assembled. We strongly recommend you to stick some gummed brown paper tape on to the overlaps before you trim them as this will minimise the risk of the veneer splitting.

If you are using a contact adhesive the job is straightforward, and about the only difficulty is making sure that no air is trapped underneath; the best way to avoid this is to insert a piece of waxed paper between the veneer and the groundwork and gradually withdraw it as you press the veneer down.

With all other kinds of adhesive, however, the necessity for some form of cramping becomes paramount, and it is this that makes veneering curved shapes so difficult. There are three ways of applying pressure – by employing cauls, by sandbags, or by a vacuum bag.

Cauls are blocks of wood (usually softwood) which are made to the reverse shape of the work being veneered. If you are using Scotch glue, the method is to heat the cauls, but only to the degree when they can still be handled, and then cramp the work between them; for adhesives other than Scotch glue, they can be used cold. The principal disadvantage is that they frequently need to be quite large and take a long time to prepare – in other words, they are suited to repetition work but not to 'one-offs'.

The way to use sandbags is shown in Fig 97. The wooden box is merely a container and need not be elaborate provided its joints are strong enough to withstand pressure. The sandbags can be linen or a double thickness of cotton, or any non-fibrous fabric; plastic bags are not suitable as they are usually not robust enough and tend to burst. The sand should be soft and capable of retaining an impression, and it must be bone-dry.

The procedure is to make the wooden box and its lid of such a size as will contain the sandbags and the work; the upper bag should bulge slightly above the level of the top so that when the lid is screwed or cramped down the sand is forced hard against the veneer and the curves of the work; the whole thing can then be left until the adhesive has set. If you are using Scotch glue you must heat the sand before putting it in the bag so that the glue is not chilled; before veneering, press the work into the sandbag to get a good impression and then remove the work and put the box with the impressed sand into a cooker

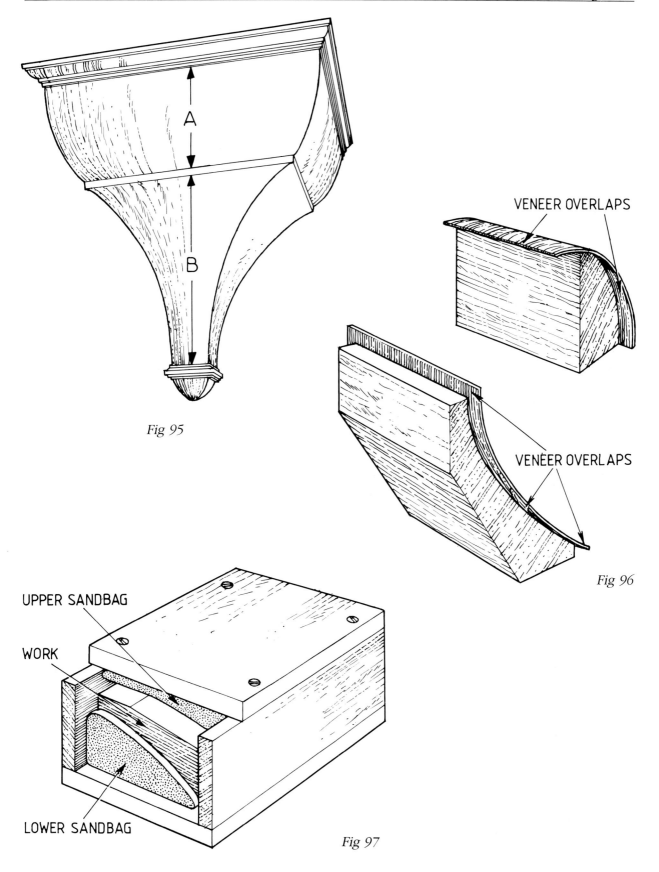

Fig 95

VENEER OVERLAPS

VENEER OVERLAPS

Fig 96

UPPER SANDBAG

WORK

LOWER SANDBAG

Fig 97

oven on the slowest heat. You will have to judge for yourself how long to leave it, but as a guide you should be able to handle the box with bare hands. When it is right, put in the work and the veneer and screw or clamp down the lid.

A vacuum bag is a flexible rubber bag which can be connected to a vacuum pump; when the pump is switched on it exhausts the air very quickly, pulling the bag snugly around whatever is in it. If you have thoughts of using a plastic bag and an ordinary domestic vacuum cleaner you are in for a disappointment as, first, the thickest plastic is not strong enough and all too often splits and, second, a domestic cleaner is not sufficiently powerful. Vacuum bags are made commercially but it is not too difficult to make efficient equipment for yourself. If you do, be sure to use a bag material such as 2mm ($\frac{1}{16}$in) sheet rubber, or the special Neoprene-coated nylon from which inflatable boats are made, plus a vacuum pump which will exhaust the air speedily and down to below 1lb per sq in (0.07kg per sq cm). You can avoid puncturing the bag by placing thick wads of newspaper over any sharp edges or projections on the work.

◇ HAMMER-VENEERING ◇

This is not a common way of laying veneers as modern synthetic adhesives are not suitable. Hammer-veneering calls for an adhesive which has an initial bond sufficient to hold the veneer in position while the hammer is being used – only freshly made Scotch glue (see Appendix ii) is acceptable to do the job properly, and it should run off the brush without separating into drops.

Fig 98A shows a hammer that you can make; Fig 98B a proprietary hammer; and Fig 98C an electrically heated model. The last-named is particularly valuable as it avoids the need to use an electric iron on the veneer to warm the glue. Our own hammer (Fig 99) was made in the workshop and you will see that instead of a metal blade it has a wooden one, which is less likely to bruise the work.

The procedure is to brush plenty of glue into both the groundwork and the underside of the veneer, and then place the veneer in position with your fingers and press it down. Next, wipe over half its area with a damp cloth; do not wet the veneer too much but just leave a film of moisture to prevent the electric iron scorching it. The iron should be set at its lowest heat, which will soften the glue. Pass it lightly over the dampened area and then place the hammer firmly on one end of the veneer midway across the panel. Work it forwards, along the grain if possible, in a zigzag motion by pivoting it on each end of the blade alternately. Repeat the procedure across the panel, working outwards to both edges to exclude excess air and glue.

If the veneer persists in bubbling at any point you can cramp a small block of wood over it with a piece of plastic film or paper interposed between the block and the veneer. Sometimes a bubble appears in the centre of the panel and is inaccessible to cramps, and in this case you can place a metal tool such as a power-drill on it as the cold metal will chill the glue and cause it to set quickly.

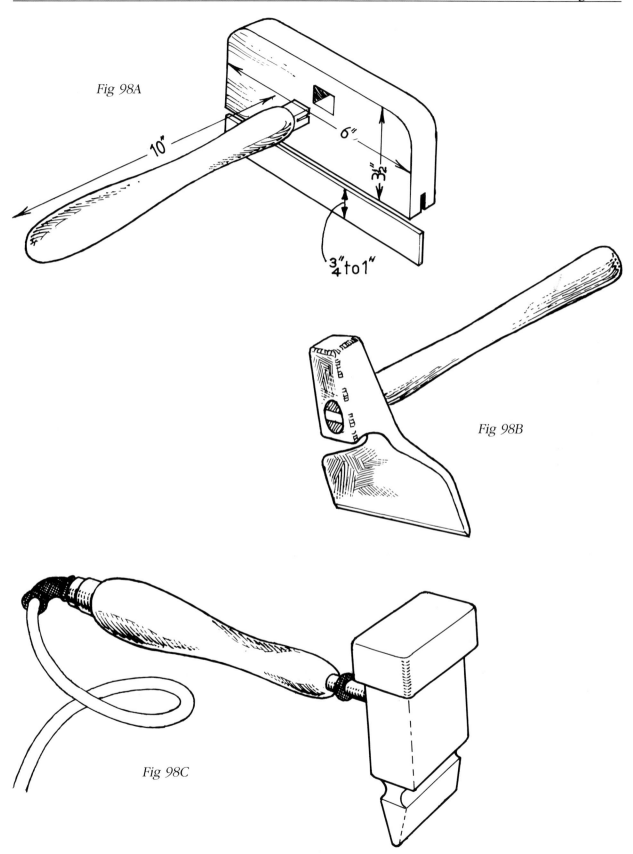

Fig 98A

10"

6"

3½"

¾"to1"

Fig 98B

Fig 98C

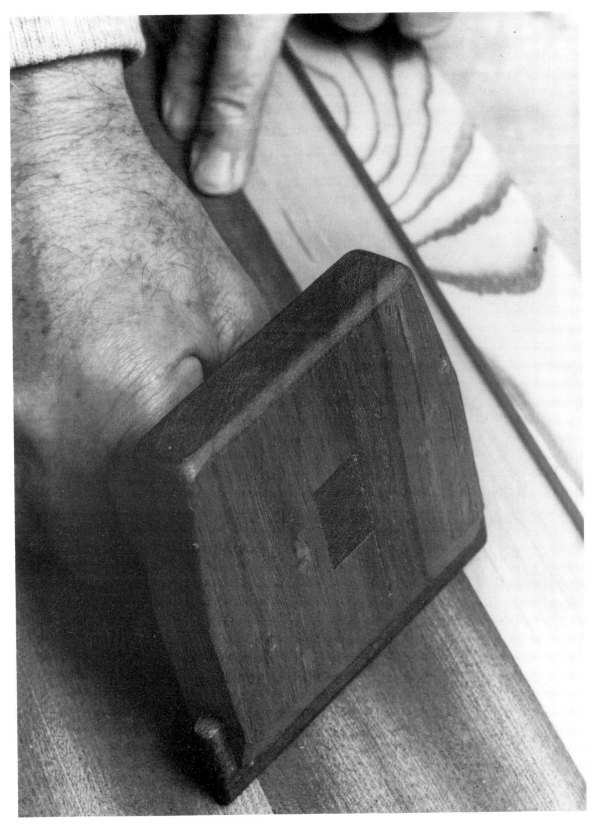

Fig 99

◇ MAKING FANS ◇

Fans come in two styles; convex, as shown in Fig 100C, and the spandrel design in Fig 100D. They are made in a similar fashion.

The first task is to cut or saw the tapered pieces and then fit them together, having shaded the edges by holding each one in a pair of tweezers and dipping one edge in hot sand contained in a metal tray. Having assembled the pieces as shown in Fig 100A, hold them together with a strip of gummed brown-paper tape; do not use pressure-sensitive tapes such as Sellotape or Scotch tape as they do not always adhere well and, if they do, you can easily pull off slivers of veneer when removing them.

You can now proceed in either of two ways. One is to put the darker veneer parts together with the assembled fan and cut through both with a fine fretsaw – this is the recommended method if you are using saw-cut veneers. However, if knife-cut veneers are involved, you can cramp the

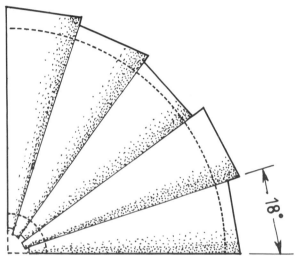

Fig 100A

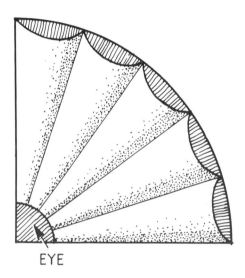

Fig 100C

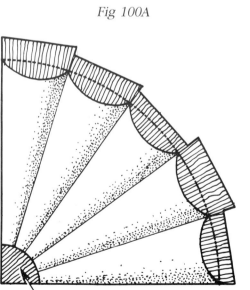

Fig 100B

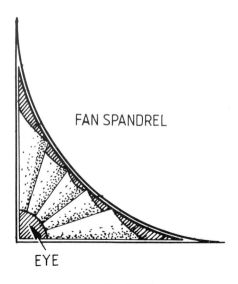

Fig 100D

assembled fan on to a block as shown in Fig 100E and chop out the curved hollows with a sharp scribing gouge; pieces of the darker veneer can then be cut and fitted up to them. The eyes can be dealt with in the same way.

The final job is to fit a boxwood or ebony line around the curve, and you can do this by cramping a block of scrapwood over the assembled fan and bending and gluing the inlay line around the curve, holding the line in place by veneer pins partly driven in around the outside edge.

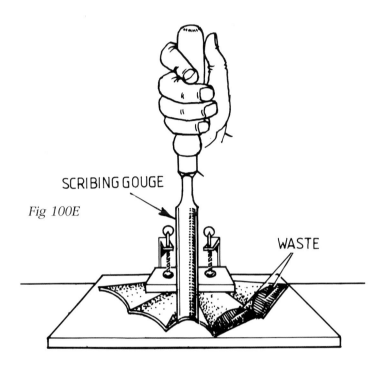

SCRIBING GOUGE

WASTE

Fig 100E

◇ MAKING BANDINGS ◇

This is a particularly satisfying job as you can achieve some fascinating results quite simply and have the added bonus of using up pieces of scrap timber.

The principle is to glue pieces of cross-grained wood together, mounting them on a baseboard either side by side or on top of one another, but in both cases with the end grain showing. Make a block at least 18mm (¾in) thick and 300mm (11¾in) wide, Fig 101A. Plane one face true, and then square off one edge from it, ideally using a TCT circular saw-blade. Next, cut off a section and prepare the outer layers from wood which matches the job you are working on. They can then be glued to the end grain of the core (Fig 101B) and when the glue has set, the face can be planed and slices of the required thickness can be cut off with a fine saw (Fig 101C) allowing a little extra for cleaning off.

WAXED PAPER OR PLASTIC FILM

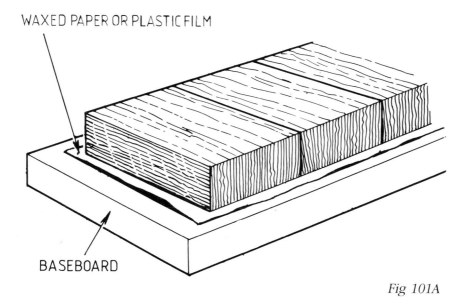

BASEBOARD

Fig 101A

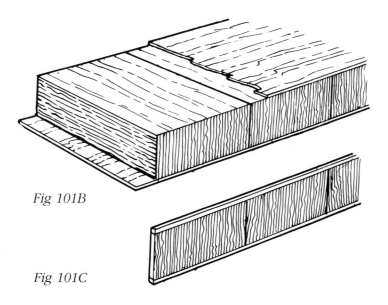

Fig 101B

Fig 101C

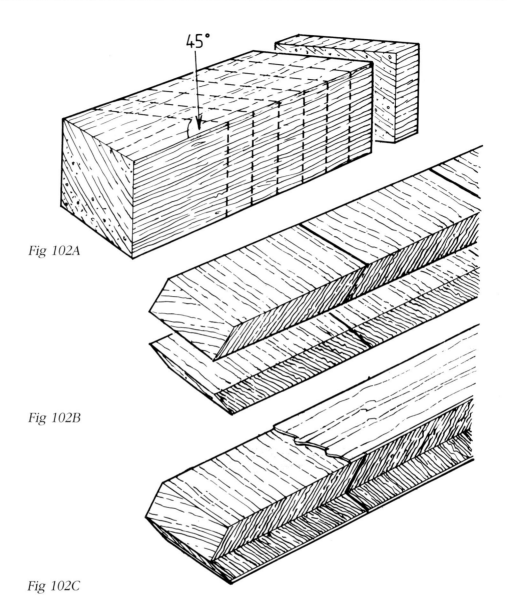

Fig 102A

Fig 102B

Fig 102C

Herringbone bandings are made in a similar fashion. Strips of equal thickness are cut across the wood at an angle of 45 degrees (Fig 102A). They are then glued together (Fig 102B), sandwiched between outer veneers (Fig 102C), and the slices are cut off.

The suggested sizes are for working on a machine; smaller pieces can be worked by hand but might be dangerous if attempted on a machine. Fig 103 shows a selection of finished bandings, together with some in preparation.

Fig 103

10 Workshop Geometry and Projects

It is an unfortunate fact of the woodworker's life that sooner or later he becomes involved with problems of geometry, most of which are pretty basic. Now and again a rather more complicated problem crops up, clock-case making having its fair share of them, and the following are some of the commonest.

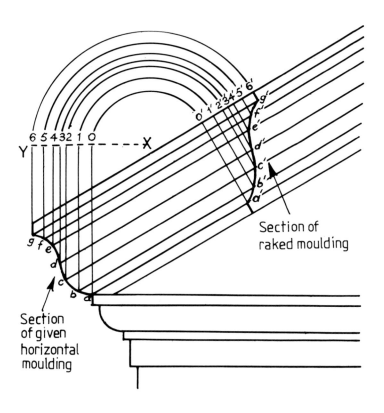

Section of raked moulding

Section of given horizontal moulding

◇ ENTASIS IN COLUMNS ◇

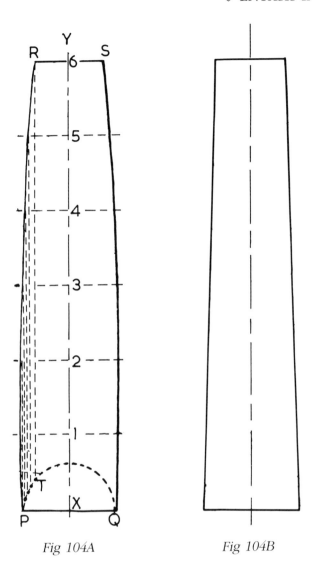

Columns are usually slightly tapered in their height and if they are left as plain cylinders (Fig 104B) they have a rather unfinished and crude look about them. This was recognised by the ancient Greeks, who introduced a feature called 'entasis' – a slight swelling which greatly improved the appearance of the columns.

Fig 104A shows how to calculate the amount and position of the entasis. Begin by drawing the vertical centre-line XY and mark in the ends PQ and RS; then draw a semicircle with its centre at X, its diameter being PQ. Drop a perpendicular down from R to cut the semicircle at T and divide the arc PT into a convenient number of parts – we have shown six (Fig 104C). Divide the vertical line XY into the same number of parts and draw horizontal lines across at each intersection; then draw verticals from each numbered point on the semicircle to the corresponding horizontal line drawn through the vertical centre-line. Thus, point 5 on the semicircle is drawn upwards to intersect the horizontal line numbered 5, and so on; the enlarged detail in the inset drawing Fig 104C will make this clear. Finally, join up all the points of intersection and this will give you the correct entasis.

Fig 104A

Fig 104B

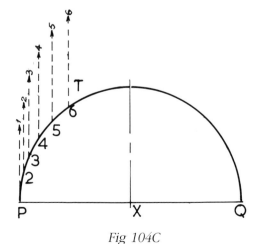

Fig 104C

◇ MITRES ON CURVED MOULDINGS ◇

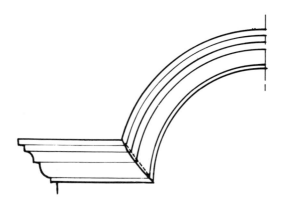

Fig 105A

When a straight length of moulding meets a curved piece which has the same profile, as in Fig 105A, you will have to choose between altering the profile of one of the pieces to match the other, or using a curved mitre. The latter course is obviously better, as altering the profile involves a lot of work.

The method of marking out a curved mitre is shown in Fig 105B. Draw the straight moulding full size, inserting all the members – if the moulding is a continuous curve with no members, put in one or two reference lines. Next, draw the curved moulding, spacing the members (or reference lines) to be identical with those on the straight moulding. The easiest way to do this is to place a strip of paper across the straight moulding at right angles and mark off the members or reference lines. Position the paper strip radially across the curve, transfer the marked points, and draw in the curved members; you will thus obtain a series of intersection points which, when joined up freehand, will give you the curve of the mitre. In the illustration the dotted line is straight and serves to emphasise the curve of the mitre.

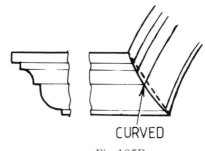

CURVED

Fig 105B

◇ INTERSECTION OF RAKED MOULDINGS ◇

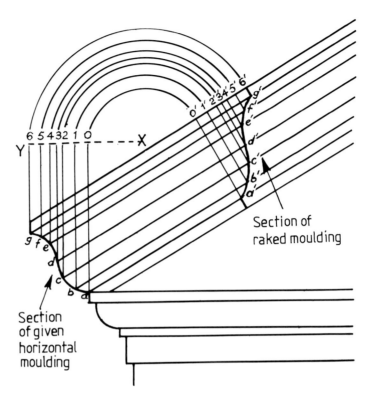

Fig 106A

A 'raked' moulding is one which is pitched at an angle to the horizontal, and for our purposes it is best exemplified by a pediment, as shown in Fig 106B, which has a horizontal return moulding at each end.

You have to find the correct profile for the raked portion of moulding so that it will match up with that of the horizontal moulding of the return. Start by drawing the profile of the latter (Fig 106A) and marking reference points (a, b, c, d, e, f, g) on to it; the number of points can be any that is convenient for your purpose. Having marked them and extended them by parallel lines along the moulding, erect perpendiculars from each one to meet the line XY at 0, 1, 2, 3, 4, 5 and 6 respectively. This line can, again, be located to suit your convenience. With a pair of compasses and using X as the centre, draw a series of arcs to intersect the raked moulding at 0', 1', 2',

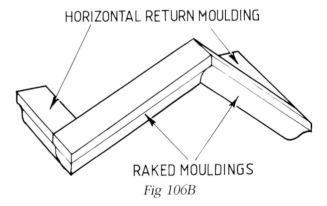

Fig 106B

3', 4', 5' and 6'. Then draw parallel lines from each of these points at right angles to the raked mouldings; the line from 6' is drawn to intersect at g'; 5' to intersect at f'; and so on. These intersection points can then be joined with a freehand curve which will give the required profile.

◇ MARKING OUT BEVELLED CAPPINGS ◇

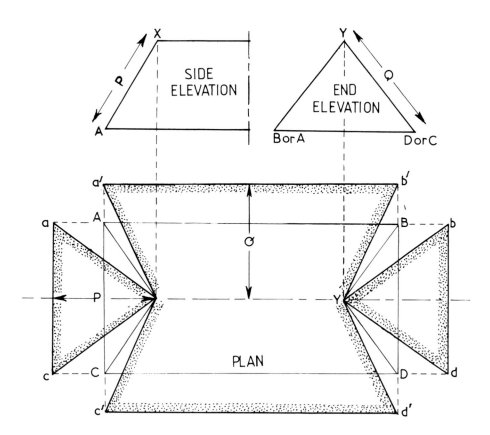

Fig 107A

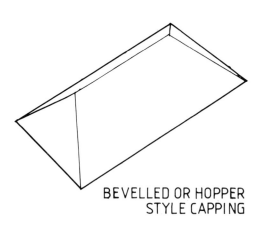

BEVELLED OR HOPPER
STYLE CAPPING

Fig 107B

These involve the treatment of compound angles, which are formed when lines which slope away in two planes simultaneously meet each other; they are shaded in the inset diagram in Fig 107. Obvious examples in everyday life are hipped roofs, hoppers, and the bodies of wheelbarrows.

The first step is to draw the side elevation AX, the end elevation BDY, and the plan ABCD; all are shown in Fig 107A. Next, draw the line ac on the plan parallel to AC at a distance P from point X, which is an apex; the distance P equals the length AX on the side elevation. Similarly, draw the line a'b' parallel to AB at a distance Q from the line XY; distance Q equals DY on the end elevation. The lengths of ac and a'b' are determined by extending the lines AB and CD, and AC and BD respectively. This gives you the size and shape of the parts (shown shaded) and when these are laid on your timber and cut to shape they can be assembled to form the capping, Fig 107B.

◇ MARKING OUT CONVEX CAPPINGS ◇

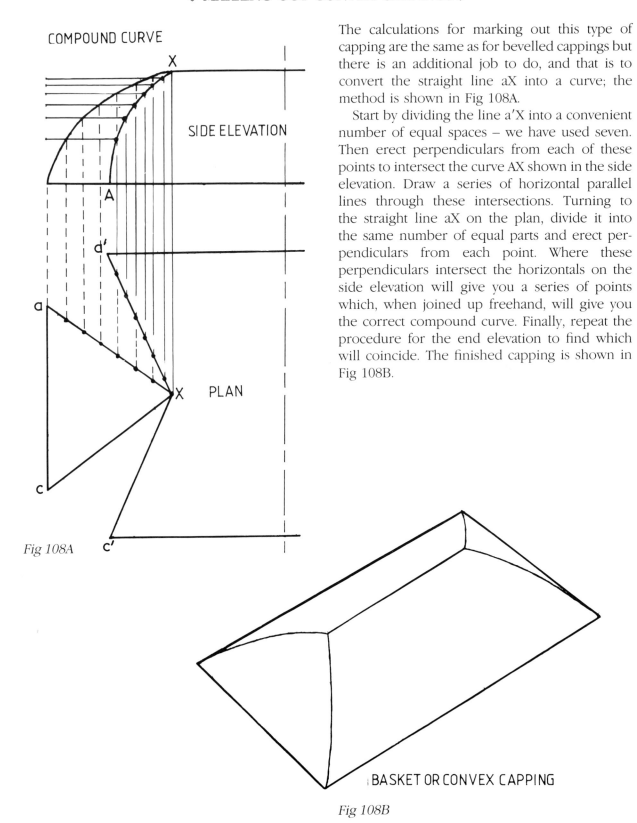

COMPOUND CURVE

X

SIDE ELEVATION

A

d'

a

X   PLAN

c

Fig 108A   c'

The calculations for marking out this type of capping are the same as for bevelled cappings but there is an additional job to do, and that is to convert the straight line aX into a curve; the method is shown in Fig 108A.

Start by dividing the line a'X into a convenient number of equal spaces – we have used seven. Then erect perpendiculars from each of these points to intersect the curve AX shown in the side elevation. Draw a series of horizontal parallel lines through these intersections. Turning to the straight line aX on the plan, divide it into the same number of equal parts and erect perpendiculars from each point. Where these perpendiculars intersect the horizontals on the side elevation will give you a series of points which, when joined up freehand, will give you the correct compound curve. Finally, repeat the procedure for the end elevation to find which will coincide. The finished capping is shown in Fig 108B.

BASKET OR CONVEX CAPPING

Fig 108B

◇ PLOTTING SPIRALS ◇

The difference between a helix and a spiral is explained on page 161; now we come to the method of plotting a spiral. You may find this useful when you are inlaying lines or marking out a pattern for marquetry.

We have broken the process down into three stages in Fig 109.

The first step (Fig 109A) is to draw the circle which contains the spiral and divide it into twelve equal sections; you can use a protractor to measure off twelve 30-degree angles, or a 30/60 angled set-square. Next, divide the vertical radius from the centre X into twelve equal parts.

Taking the compasses, and using the point X as centre, draw an arc from point 1 to the vertical radius 1, then another arc from point 2 to radius 2, and so on (Fig 109B). In Fig 109C, the points of intersection are joined up freehand to give the spiral.

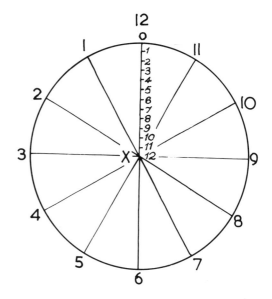

Fig 109A

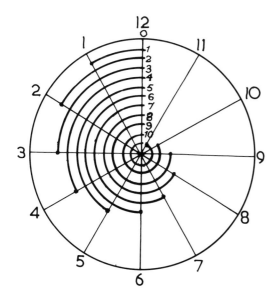

Fig 109B

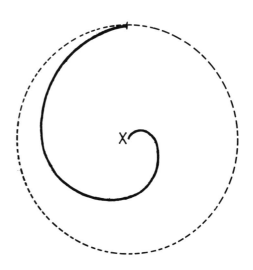

Fig 109C

Workshop Projects

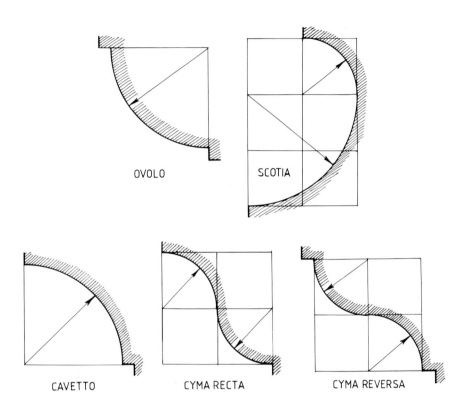

OVOLO

SCOTIA

CAVETTO

CYMA RECTA

CYMA REVERSA

◇ MAKING AND FIXING DENTIL AND GOTHIC-STYLE MOULDINGS ◇

Both kinds of moulding are often found on clock cases, and are shown in Fig 110A and B. The dentil moulding was very occasionally carved in the solid but was more usually cut out separately and glued in place; the hollow Gothic moulding was always made on its own and then glued on.

Fig 111 shows the method for making a dentil moulding; either a machine saw or a hand back saw can be used. In both cases it is simply a matter of sawing a series of cuts and chopping out the blind ends with a mortise chisel (for square ends) or a carver's gouge (for rounded ends). There is only one tool you can employ for the Gothic moulding and that is a fretsaw, either machine or hand; the small drop terminals are split turnings and are glued on to butt against the moulding once the latter has been fixed.

Although making the mouldings is straight-forward enough, a couple of snags arise when it comes to polishing and fixing them. One is that it is obviously difficult, if not impossible, to polish neatly into the crevices of the mouldings. The old-time craftsmen used first to polish the surface on which the moulding was to be fixed; the moulding was then laid on the surface once the polish was hard, and marked around its edges. It was then removed and the polish laboriously scraped away from the marked areas so that the glue would adhere to the bare wood – it would not, of course, bond to a polished surface.

We agree that this is the principle to adopt, but suggest an improvement. Instead of scraping away the polish, which is a soul destroying job, use a masking fluid. This can be bought from any store selling artist's materials, and acts as a resist to the polish; it has two decided advantages in that it does not take more than a few minutes to dry, and it can easily be peeled off by rubbing with a finger. Application is easy, too, as you simply paint it on with an artist's brush.

Another snag is that if you are using Scotch glue to stick the moulding, some of it is bound to squeeze out and look unsightly as well as being difficult to remove. So the old-timers used what was known as a 'sticking plate'. This was a strip of metal plate which was kept warm to prevent the glue chilling; it was given a thin coat of glue and the moulding was then placed on it and drawn backwards as shown in Fig 112. This ensured an even coat of glue and avoided any accumulation at the edges.

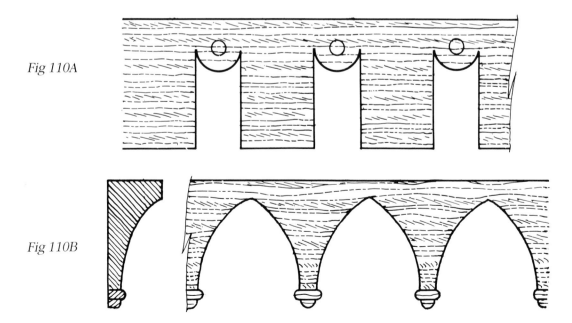

Fig 110A

Fig 110B

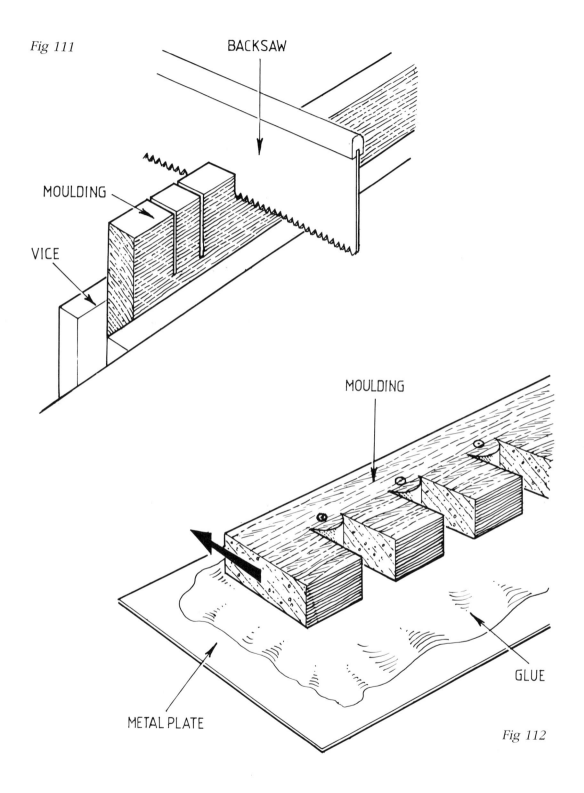

Fig 111

BACKSAW

MOULDING

VICE

MOULDING

METAL PLATE

GLUE

Fig 112

◇ MOULDING DESIGNS ◇

Designing mouldings is often a headache for clock-case makers and cabinet makers alike. We explain here some of the mysteries which surround the subject.

There are five principal designs of mouldings: the ovolo, the scotia, the cavetto, the cyma recta, and the cyma reversa (these last two are also called 'ogee' mouldings).

Each of these moulding designs was interpreted in different ways by the Romans and the ancient Greeks, as can be seen from a study of their styles of architecture. The Romans based their designs on the square, the Greeks on either ellipses or parabolic conic sections. The prob-

able reason for this is that the Romans were not mathematically inclined (as one can well appreciate when trying to use their system of numerals for anything but the simplest mathematical problems); the Greeks, however, were enthusiastic mathematicians and were, indeed, the founders of Euclidean geometry. Greek designs were used in Europe much earlier than in Britain, and it could be said that until the late seventeenth century most British mouldings were based on the Roman designs. This gave them a more sturdy and compact appearance than their continental counterparts, which were often flamboyant to the point of being grotesque.

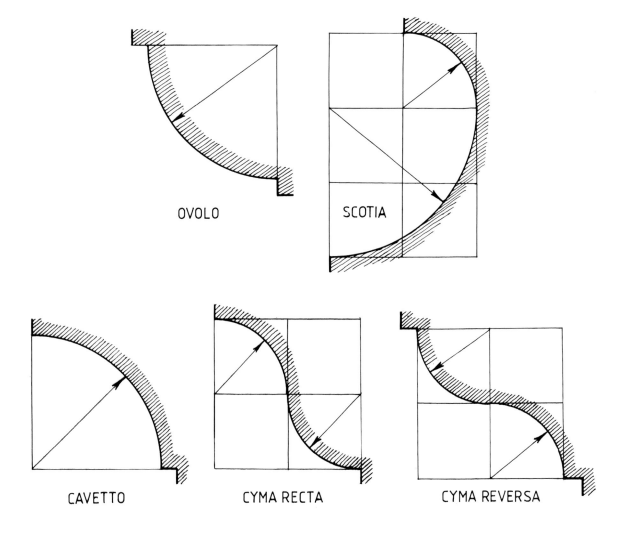

Fig 113

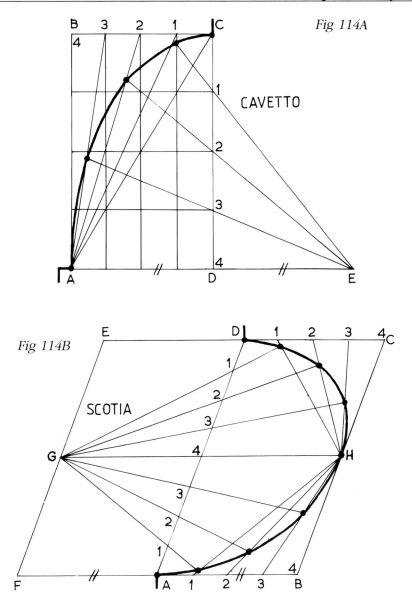

Fig 114A

CAVETTO

Fig 114B

SCOTIA

Fig 113 illustrates the five basic designs drawn in accordance with the Roman principle, and these should be self-explanatory. Fig 114 shows the Greek designs and these are a very different proposition, calling for some knowledge of geometry. An ovolo moulding is not shown in Fig 114 as it is the same in both styles, being a quadrant of a circle.

Fig 114A shows a cavetto design; the rectangle containing the curve has the longer side CD, and the shorter side BC, divided into four equal parts respectively (though you can use any number

that is convenient). The base line AD is extended to E so that AD equals DE, and reference lines are drawn from E through each of the subdividing points on CD. A diagonal is drawn from A to C, followed by a series of reference lines from A to the subdividing points on BC. Where the reference lines intersect gives you a series of points which can be joined up freehand to create the cavetto curve.

The scotia design (Fig 114B) is plotted in a similar fashion. The scotia is inscribed in the parallelogram ABCD, with H as the half-way point

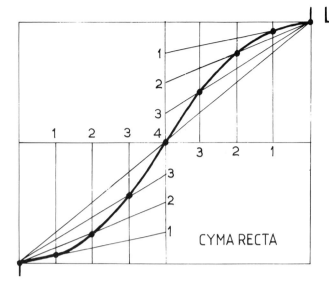

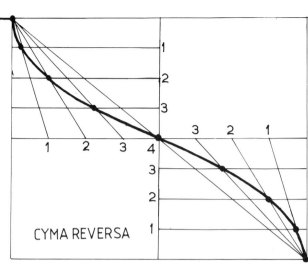

Fig 115

on BC; AB is extended to F so that AB equals AF, and CD is extended to E so that DC equals DE; H is joined to G. Next, AB and CD are subdivided into four equal parts, and AD into eight. Refer-

ence lines are drawn from H and G respectively and their points of intersection enable you to draw the curve.

The two cymas, recta and reversa, are illustrated in Fig 115, and follow the same method as for the cavetto and scotia designs.

◇ PELLETING ◇

Pellets are small plugs which can be used to fill the cavities over the heads of wood screws, small knot-holes, or blemishes. Fig 116 shows a series of pellets that have been turned on the lathe but not yet separated; this method is suitable only for large pellets, as turning cross grain can be tricky (not to say dangerous) in small diameters. Note that the essential difference between a pellet and a plug is that a pellet is formed so that its head shows long grain which can be aligned to the grain of the work, while a plug is simply a short length cut off a dowel, or a similar kind of rod, and thus shows end grain.

However, there is an easy and safe alternative to turning them on the lathe, and that is to buy a

plug cutter which can be used in a power tool. This cuts a pellet very quickly; if you use an offcut from the wood you are working with, the grain will be certain to match.

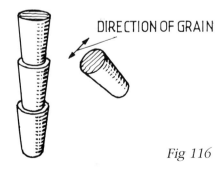

Fig 116

◇ MAKING TWIST COLUMNS ◇

Twist columns are frequently used in longcase hoods and also as decorative features in other kinds of clocks. Provided that you follow the correct sequence of operations and take care to be accurate at each stage, you will find the job straightforward and the result satisfying.

Before starting on the practicalities, we must first of all deal with the theory of 'pitch'. The best way to understand pitch is to visualise a nut travelling along the threads of a bolt; as the nut rotates around the bolt it travels forward a certain length, and the distance it covers in one complete revolution is the pitch. As shown in Fig 117 the pitch depends on the angle of the threads. From our point of view, the general rule is that the pitch should be approximately equal to the diameter of the column, but this is only a guide and you can alter it to suit your own requirements.

A few words are needed to clarify some nomenclature. Many people talk of a spiral when they really mean a helix; it is not as pedantic as it may seem to emphasise the difference between them, as both are met with in woodwork. The spiral is exemplified by the volutes sometimes used in classical decoration, and the helix by the

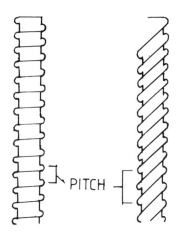

Fig 117

ordinary twist leg. Basically, a spiral is the path of a point which revolves around a central axis and eventually meets it; a helix is also the path of a point which revolves around a central axis but the path and the axis, being parallel, never meet. Both are shown in Fig 118.

The next thing to be decided on is the depth of the hollowed-out groove; Fig 119 should help you. If you make the groove so deep as to cut nearly half-way through the wood you will get a graceful but inherently weak example as in Fig

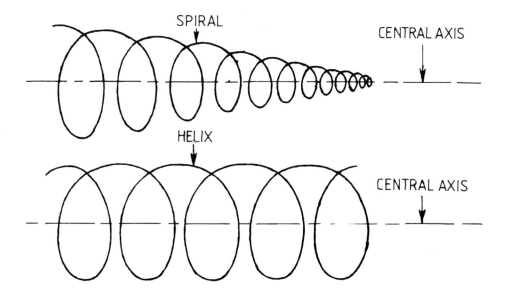

Fig 118

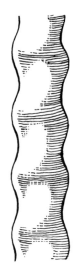

Fig 119A   *Fig 119B*   *Fig 119C*

119A; if you go to the other extreme and cut only a shallow groove, the result will be something like Fig 119B and will be a rather characterless specimen. So it is a case of compromising between the two, as shown in Fig 119C. However, you must take into account the work the column has to do and, if it is for decorative purposes only, the example in Fig 119A could be the most suitable one. All three illustrations have the same pitch, as this is not affected by the depth of the grooves except in very exaggerated designs. Finally, do not forget to pair the twists, one left-hand and one right-hand, to achieve a nicely balanced effect on the hood.

You do not necessarily need a lathe to make twist columns, although obviously it is a great help. The basic requirement is a cylinder on which to mark out the helix, and whether you turn it on a lathe or plane and shape it up by hand is immaterial.

Fig 120 shows a blank that has been turned with a square at each end to enable the work to be held easily in a vice. If you have turned the column instead of planing it you cannot do this, but you can screw a square block to each end of the cylinder; the screw holes will not show, of course, when the column comes to be fixed in place. Mark up the ends as shown in Fig 120A and draw four lines from end to end. Cut a piece of thin card which is the same width as the diameter of the column and of such a length that it just

wraps around the column; this can then be employed as a template to mark a series of rings along the column.

Mark the central point between each ring, and then mark two other points, X and Y, each 5mm ($\frac{3}{16}$in) away from the original central point. Next, fix a length of adhesive tape, 10mm ($\frac{3}{8}$in) wide would be suitable, at one end of the column, either by sticking it down or with a drawing pin, and wind it around the column as shown by the dotted lines; pencil in a firm line along the opposite edges of the tape, which can then be removed. This will leave you with the column marked as shown in Fig 120B; it is a good idea to scribble pencil lines between the helix so that you can see just what has to be cut away.

Start shaping the groove by scoring along the pencilled lines of the helix, and then follow on with a woodcarver's gouge, assisted by any kind of chisel which seems to be appropriate! You will find a rasp or shaper tool of the Surform type invaluable, too. Obviously you will have to keep turning the work in the vice to expose a new face as you progress. The edges of the groove have to be rounded off, and a small chisel followed by a rasp should make a good job of this. Finish off by glasspapering in the usual way.

Fig 121 shows (left), the cylinder taped up; (right) the finished twist; also the type and size of gouge used for shaping the twist.

Fig 120A

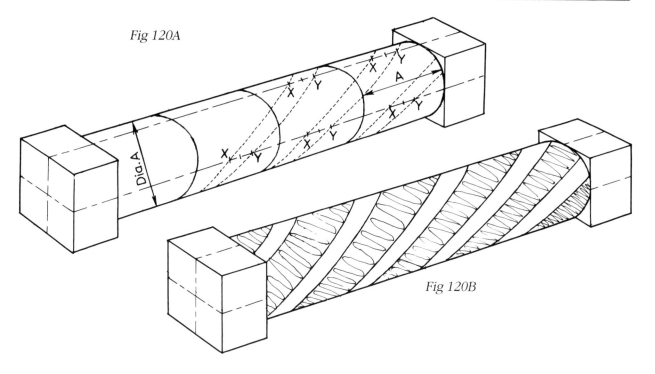

Fig 120B

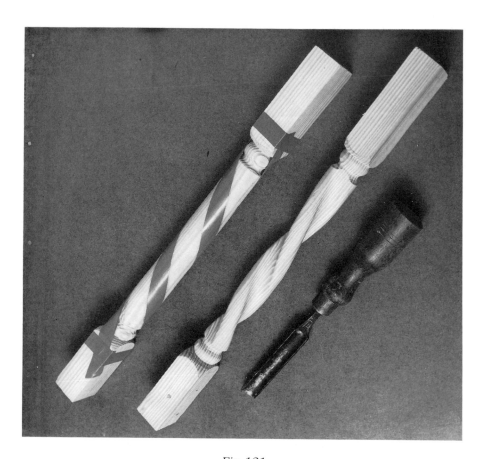

Fig 121

◇ MAKING FLUTED AND REEDED COLUMNS ◇

The same method is used to form flutes or reeds, regardless of the shape of the column from end to end. Turn the column on the lathe to the shape that you have decided upon, leaving a projecting pin on each end – take care to make the pins the same diameter as it makes it easier to hold the column steady in the jig.

Making the jig is quite simple, and a completed one with the column in place is shown in Fig 122. Its base can be any oddment of wood, block-board, stout plywood, or even chipboard. The two sides need to be a little wider than the column thickness and 150mm (6in) or so longer. For the end clamps use two blocks of any hard-wood 25mm (1in) larger than the column dia-

meter and 6mm (¼in) wider. Bore a hole the same size as the pins through the centre of each block; then saw the blocks in two, at a point one-quarter of the diameter of the hole down from one side. The larger pieces are then fixed between the sides, forming a cradle for the pins to rest in. The smaller pieces can next be drilled and screwed to the lower sections to hold the work steady while routing the flutes or reeds, after the sides and ends have been secured to the base. Also, it's a good plan to fix stops on the outside of the jig sides which will contact the router fence or guide and prevent it from going too far and damaging either the base or the cap of the column. Make small saw cuts on the top edges of each of the end clamps to act as register marks; they should be located centrally over the pins.

Fig 122

Fig 123

The spacing of the flutes is critical as the periphery must be divided accurately into equal divisions so that the last cut reaches, but does not over-run, the edge of the first cut. Mark the divisions carefully around the columns, clear of the cuts so that the division marks can be aligned with the register marks on the jig.

Insert the appropriate cutter in your router and fit the fence or guide to it; the latter should be set up so that when touching the outside of the jig, the cutter is positioned centrally over the register mark, Fig 123. Start the flute with a shallow cut and lower the cutter in easy stages to arrive at the exact width.

◇ FIXING GLASS ◇

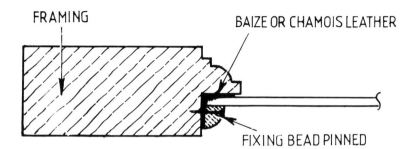

FRAMING

BAIZE OR CHAMOIS LEATHER

FIXING BEAD PINNED

Fig 124

Fig 124 shows how the glass sits in a rabbet on the inside of the framing and is held in place by a small beading which is pinned (not glued) to the frame, so that if the glass should need replacing you only need to prise off the beading, put in the new glass, and re-pin the beading into place. What may be new to some readers is the inclusion of a narrow strip of baize or chamois leather in the rabbet, and the purpose of this is two-fold. First, it helps to absorb any shock so that if, say, a glazed door is slammed, the resulting vibration of the wood is absorbed to a certain extent and is not transmitted to the glass; second, the thickness of the material will take up minor imperfections in the rabbet, including any tiny particles of sawdust which might be present. Anyone who has fitted a sheet of glass to a wood frame will confirm that it is only too easy for glass to shatter if it is pressed into a frame that is not quite flat or which has collected a little dust. The baize or chamois-leather strip does not show, of course, being hidden on one side by the rabbet and on the other by the beading.

Another method is to fix the glass into place with putty which has a small quantity of gold size (from art dealers) added to it; this sets extremely hard. The first step is to hold the glass in place with a few small veneer pins tapped in as in Fig 125 – ordinary glazing sprigs can be used if they are not too big. The easiest way to tap them in is with the edge of a firmer chisel (bevel down-

wards) which is slid sideways on the face of the glass (Fig 125).

To make the putty, take a small handful of ordinary putty as used for glazing wooden window frames and make a depression with your thumb. Fill the depression with gold size and knead the putty in the usual way before use. There is also a proprietary mastic adhesive which is made for the job; it comes in various colours, has the consistency of putty, and has the added advantage of permanent elasticity which enables it to absorb vibration.

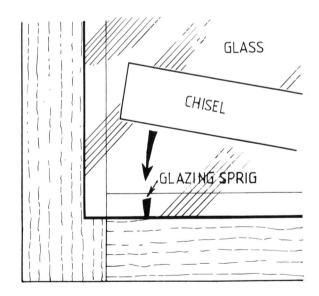

GLASS

CHISEL

GLAZING SPRIG

Fig 125

◇ MAKING FIELDED PANELS ◇

A fielded panel is one which has its edges bevelled all round; the bevelled edges fit into grooves worked on the inner faces of the panel framing and, as the panel is never glued in but left dry, it is free to shrink or swell without the movement being obvious. This means that a fielded panel should at least have its edges stained, if not polished, before assembly, otherwise it will show raw wood edges if and when it shrinks. Fig 126A shows the section; note that a small gap of about 2mm (1/16in) is left all round to allow for any swelling that may occur. Fig 126B shows the section used by the old-time craftsmen – the bevelled portion is dished so that it can move even more freely.

Assuming that you are going to use a power router you will need a set-up like that shown in Fig 127, in which the sloped fielding is packed up so that it will be horizontal as the routing is undertaken. The edge marked 'trim here' will need to be trimmed by hand to be at right angles to the face of the panel, as the router will cut it at an angle. It is strongly recommended that you use a 'plunge' router so that you can pre-set it and avoid the kick which often happens with an ordinary router when it touches the wood.

Fielding can also be worked by hand, and can be on one or both sides of the panel, as desired. The single-sided fielding is simpler and needs one shallow rabbet at the top of the bevel, which

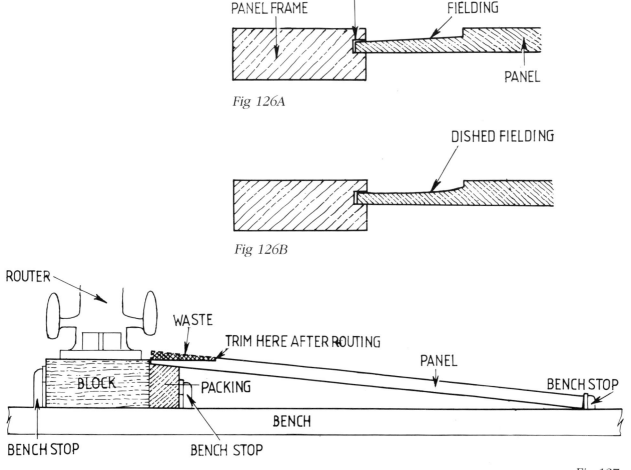

Fig 126A

Fig 126B

Fig 127

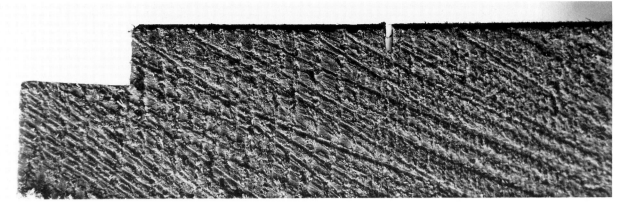

Fig 128A

Fig 128B

Fig 128C

Fig 128D

is then worked to the outer edge of the panel in one operation. The method shown in Fig 128A, B, C and D is for the double-sided kind, and is more involved. The outer edges do not carry the bevel but are worked on the same plane as the panel face otherwise the edges become too thin and are liable to break away if knocked.

Having decided the width of bevel which is best suited to the size of the door, mark out the face panel with a sharp marking knife to give clean edges to the rabbets, particularly across the grain. Fig 128A shows how to form the outer edge with a rabbet plane after sawing to the required depth across the grain at the ends; you can then work along the sides without sawing. Fig 128B shows how to carry on with the shallow sinking at the top edge of the bevel, working in the same way. Fig 128C illustrates the last side about to receive the bevel after the foregoing operations have been completed. Fig 128D shows the method of forming the bevel and at the same time protecting the edge on the face of the panel by using a temporary guide which is cramped on.

There is another type of fielding and Fig 129 shows a section. Instead of fitting into a groove, the fielded edges are located in rabbets, and small beads are pinned and glued on to the framing on the inside, taking care that no glue gets on to the face of the panel. The panel itself is not glued in but fitted dry.

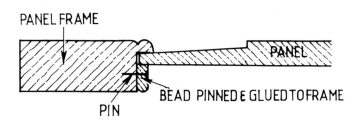

PANEL FRAME

PANEL

BEAD PINNED & GLUED TO FRAME

PIN

Fig 129

◇ MAKING INVERTED BELL-TOPS ◇

Although these are not easy to make, if you follow a logical sequence such as that shown in the sectional drawings in Figs 130A, B, C, and D, the job should be straightforward.

Starting with the square wooden blank Fig 130A, the ogee shape is worked either by a spindle-moulder, a machine router, or by hand (Fig 130B). Follow this by sawing through as shown in Fig 130C to leave the two flats indicated; you have to use your own judgement as to how wide they should be, bearing in mind that the bottom one has to be fixed to the clock case and the upper one to some form of capping. The vertical flat is important, too, and you should leave enough wood so that when the pieces are mitred and glued together there is plenty of gluing surface.

We strongly recommend you to measure all the parts to be sawn from one square wooden blank; Fig 130D, in section, shows how the finished blank is held in the mitre box. As with any moulding which has to be mitred, it is essential to hold it in the mitre box in the same stance as it will assume when it is finally assembled – otherwise you will find that the mitres will not match.

Fig 131 shows a typical bell-top with (A) the parts dismantled, and (B) with them assembled.

Fig 130A

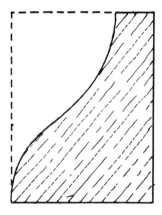

Fig 130B

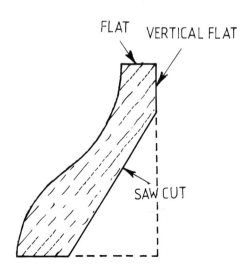

FLAT   VERTICAL FLAT

SAW CUT

Fig 130C

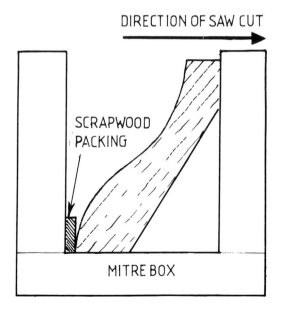

DIRECTION OF SAW CUT

SCRAPWOOD PACKING

MITRE BOX

Fig 130D

Fig 131A

Fig 131B

◇ MAKING CIRCULAR FRAMES ◇

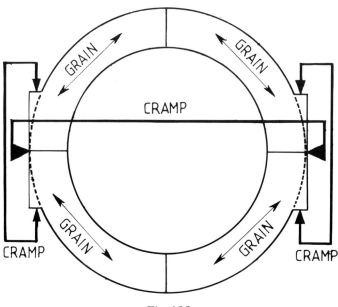

Fig 132

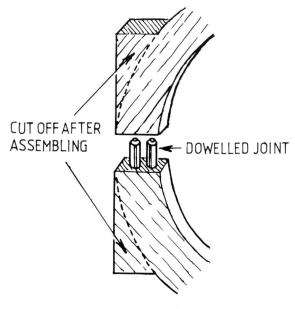

Fig 133

This is the kind of frame used for wall clocks, and there are several points to watch for.

First, ensure that the direction of the grain runs as shown by the arrows in Fig 132, as it minimises the risk of breakage due to short grain. Next, you have to give some thought to the method of cramping the segments together; Fig 133 illustrates the 'ears' or 'lugs' which can be shaped to provide good fixing for cramps. This is fine if you are bandsawing the frame, but if you are using a router to both cut it out and to round off the edge, you will find it a nuisance to stop the router in order to leave the lugs projecting. Probably the best way in this case is to rout it out completely and then cramp it with a band cramp (see page 24).

Fig 133 also shows that the joints between the segments are dowelled; this is deliberate, as mortise and tenon joints would involve short grain on either the mortise or the tenon, or both, with consequent weakness.

◇ SPLIT TURNINGS ◇

These are very popular as decorative features, and are quite simple to turn up on the lathe. Two blanks are glued together with a piece of paper between them as in Fig 134 (left). Once the glue has set, the assembly is turned in the usual way. The two halves are then separated to provide two identical half-turnings whose flat backs enable you to glue them to any flat surface (Fig 134 right).

The main points to note concern the type of paper, and the kind of adhesive to employ. Many woodworkers use a PVA (polyvinyl acetate) adhesive; if you use it for split turnings be sure to use as little as is necessary plus a soft, fairly thick wrapping paper which will not allow the adhesive to penetrate right through it, otherwise the wood and the paper will stick together and be difficult to separate.

You must also take great care to centre the work accurately in the lathe, and to locate the spur of the driving centre ACROSS the joint so that any tendency for the parts to separate is minimised.

Scotch glue is very suitable for the job as, even if it penetrates the paper, it will not matter, as it can be softened by wiping the work with warm water after turning. However, to be absolutely certain that the pieces cannot come apart while being turned, you can allow extra wood at each end and drive in wood screws to hold the pieces together; the extra wood is sawn off when the job is finished. In fact, on lengths up to, say, 230 or 250mm (9 or 10in) you can dispense with the paper and rely on the screws alone.

Fig 134

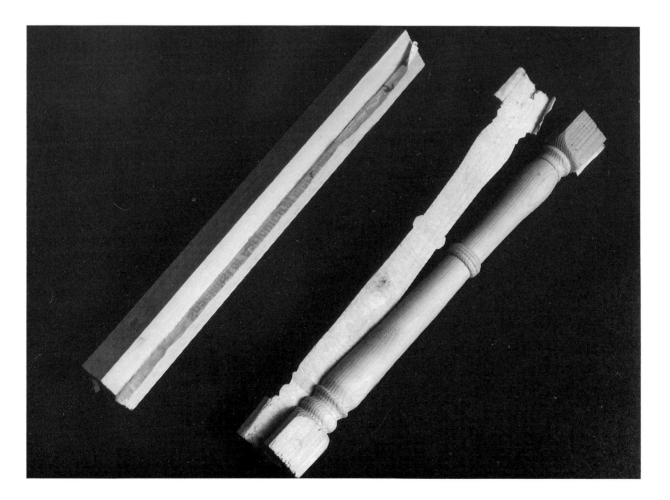

Conservation

In order to clarify the definitions of the terms 'restoration' and 'conservation', which have become synonymous, we can do no better than to quote from the guidelines laid down by the United Kingdom Institute for Conservation, as follows:

◇ THE PURPOSE OF CONSERVATION ◇

Conservation is the means by which the true nature of an object is preserved. The true nature of an object includes evidence of its origins, its original construction, and the materials of which it is composed, and information as to the technology used in its manufacture. Subsequent modifications may be of such a significant nature that they should be preserved.

In order not to change the true nature of the object, certain rules should be observed in its care and maintenance. The following describes the responsibility of the conservator to the object, since it is the conservator who has the power to preserve or distort its true nature.

The conservator and object
General obligations

All professional actions of the conservator are governed by total respect for the physical, historical, and aesthetic integrity of the object. Concern for its future should include protection against damage and loss.

One standard

With every object he or she undertakes to conserve, regardless of any opinion of its value or quality, the conservator should adhere to the highest and most exacting standard of treatment. Although circumstances may limit the extent of treatment, the quality should never be lowered. While special techniques may be required during the treatment of large groups of objects these procedures should be consistent with respect for the integrity of the individual objects.

Suitability of treatment: reversibility

The conservator should not perform or recommend any treatment which is not appropriate to the preservation of the object.

The conservator should endeavour only to use techniques and materials which, to the best of our current knowledge, will not endanger the true nature of the object, and which will not impede future treatment, or the retrieval of information through scientific examination.

The techniques and materials which affect the objects least and which can most easily and completely be reversed should always be selected. Nothing should be removed from an object without sufficient evidence that it is not part of the original condition of the object.

Examination and records

Before carrying out any treatment, the conservator should first make an adequate examination of the object and all available documentation in order to record its condition and history, and to establish the causes of its deterioration. A record of methods and materials used should be kept as a permanent, accessible archive.

Restoration

It is unethical to modify or conceal the true nature of an object through restoration.

The presence and extent of restoration must be detectable, though it need not be conspicuous. All restoration must be fully documented.

Fuller information, and details of membership, can be obtained from the United Kingdom Institute for Conservation, c/o Conservation Department, Tate Gallery, Millbank, London SW1P 4RG.

Adhesives

As Scotch glue has largely been replaced by synthetic adhesives in woodwork, it is possible that some readers have had no experience of it. Here are some guidelines if you intend to use it – indeed, you should always use it for restoration or repair on antique pieces where conservation is important (see Appendix I).

Scotch glue belongs to the class of animal glues which are made from the hides, hooves, horns, bones and other parts of animals which cannot be used by the butcher; and fish glues also come into the same category although they are used only for small jobs where strength is not important. Salisbury glue is of a particularly good quality, as it is made from animal hides only, but you will probably find it difficult to obtain.

Scotch glue is supplied in three forms: powder, 'pearl' (granules), or cake (thin sheets). If you can only get the cake type you will have to break it into small pieces and the best way to do this is to put it in a sack or bag to prevent pieces flying about and hit it with a hammer.

All types must be allowed to stand overnight in a container with just enough water to cover them. The choice of container is important as some metals will discolour the glue, and by far the best is an ovenproof glass jug or bowl. The glue will not dissolve in cold water, but it will form a jelly and this must be heated to get liquid glue. Place the container in a large saucepan of cold water, and rest the container on a small block of wood so that the water can circulate all round – the level of the water should be just below that of the glue. Heat the pan, but make sure that the temperature never exceeds 63°C (145°F), or the glue will lose its strength. The glue container must be ovenproof or it will crack.

Stir the glue gently from time to time with a piece of wooden dowel (not metal or plastic) and remove any scum which may come to the surface. To test when the glue is ready, dip in a glue-brush and then hold it up; if the glue runs off the brush in a smooth stream with no lumps and no breaking into drops, it is ready. Never make up more than you need for the job in hand as re-heated glue rapidly loses its strength.

As the glue must be used hot, it is important that the parts to be joined are hot as well, otherwise the glue will become chilled and lose its strength. How you heat the wood depends on what heat-source you have available, but you should bring the temperature of the wood parts up just enough to allow you to handle them without being scorched. It is obvious that you have to work quickly, so all cramps and other equipment should be laid out ready to hand; also, the temperature of the workshop should ideally be about 26°C (78°F).

The initial setting of the glue is fairly rapid, but complete hardening takes about ten to twelve hours (depending on the workshop temperature), and cramps should be left on for that time. The glue does not stain but has a brown glue line; if this is undesirable, you can add a small quantity of precipitated chalk or a white powder pigment. Wipe away any excess glue with a damp rag. If you need to break the joint at any future time you can do so by warming it with a rag dampened with warm water, which will liquefy the glue. Unfortunately the glue has little resistance to damp, and in such conditions joints will become loose and the glue itself may suffer fungal attack.

The following chart shows the characteristics of various kinds of adhesives – we hope it may prove useful.

	Animal	Casein	Contact	Epoxy	PVA	RF	UF
General strength	Good	Good	Very fair	Excellent	Good	Excellent	Excellent
Water resistance	Nil	Poor	Fair	Excellent	Poor	Excellent	Good
Damp resistance	Poor	Fair	Good	Excellent	Fair	Excellent	Good
Mould resistance	Poor	Fair	Good	Excellent	Good	Excellent	Excellent
Heat resistance	Nil	Good	Very fair	Excellent	Poor	Good	Good
Gap filling	Nil	Slight	Nil	Good	Nil	Good	Good
Hardening time	10–12hr	4–6hr	10–30min	5min–48hr	20–40min	6–8hr	6–8hr
Colour when dry	Light brown	Clear straw	Clear pale straw	Yellow	Clear	Opaque white	Opaque white
Liable to stain	No	Yes	No	No	No	Yes, some woods	Yes, some woods

(RF = resorcinol formaldehyde; UF = urea formaldehyde)

Wood-boring Insects

The two insects which are most likely to cause damage to clock cases and furniture are the common furniture beetle (*Anobium punctatum*) and the powder post beetle (*Lyctidae*). Furniture beetles cause the tell-tale holes which are usually the first noticeable signs of an attack; in antique pieces the holes may be manifestation of an attack which took place many years ago. One of the best ways to check whether or not the pests are still present is to look for 'frass" – the minute particles of wood dust expelled by the grubs as they bore through the wood. If the surface of the wood is upright you could lay a piece of white paper at the bottom of it and leave it for a week or two to see if any frass falls on to it; if not, you can generally assume that the infestation is an old one and no remedial action is necessary. A short account of the life history of each beetle may be helpful as there are certain times of the year when treatment will be most effective.

The female furniture beetle lays her eggs between April and August and will choose crevices or cracks in the wood surface, or even old flight holes, to lay her eggs; she will, however, avoid polished or painted surfaces. The adult beetle is about 5mm long, reddish brown to dark brown in colour, and can fly. The grubs are white, and about 5mm long, and can spend from two to four years boring galleries in the wood, after which period they burrow nearer to the surface of the wood and pupate. Pupation takes a few weeks and the young beetles bore exit holes and emerge to mate and start another generation.

Treatment consists of applying a suitable proprietary insecticide which can be brushed on the affected parts, although by far the best way is to inject it directly into the holes, using something like an oil-can with a fine nozzle – spraying with an atomiser is not likely to do much good. The best time to do all this is from early spring to late summer; two treatments should be given during this period, and another one a year later. If you are renewing any affected parts, it is a good idea to brush the new wood with the insecticide before fixing it. Genuine Cuban or Central American mahoganies are very unlikely to be attacked.

Lyctus beetles are about 6mm long and reddish brown to black in colour; they can fly and begin to emerge from the timber in April and continue to do so until the late autumn. The life-cycle from egg to beetle takes a year, the adult female laying her eggs into the pores of the grain with her ovipositor. Starch in the sapwood forms the diet for the grubs, which are white, crescent-shaped, and about 5mm long. Kiln-drying the timber is useful in reducing its starch content, thus rendering it far less liable to attack; oak, ash, elm, sweet chestnut and several imported hardwoods are normally the favoured victims.

Use a proprietary insecticide to kill the grubs; it can be brushed or sprayed on at any time of the year, but the treatment will be most effective if used during the late spring and summer.

Useful Addresses

◇ BRASSFOUNDRY ◇

Craft Materials Ltd, The Haven, Station Road, Northiam, Rye, East Sussex TN31 6QL

Charles Greville & Co Ltd, Willey Mill House, Alton Road, Farnham, Surrey GU10 5EL

G. H. Hadfield, Blackbrook Hill House, Tickow Lane, Shepshed, Loughborough, Leics LE12 9EY

Mahoney Associates, 58 Stapleton Road, Bristol, Avon BS5 0RB

Meadows & Passmore, Farningham Road, Crowborough, East Sussex TN6 2JP

R. E. Rose, FBHI, 731 Sidcup Road, Eltham, London SE9 3SA

H. E. Savill, 9 St Martin's Place, Scarborough, North Yorkshire YO11 2QH

Timecraft, 10 Edinburgh Road, Formby, Liverpool L37 6EP

H. S. Walsh & Sons Ltd, 243 Beckenham Road, Beckenham, Kent BR3 4TS

Yorkwire (Leeds) Ltd, 34 Lupton Street, Leeds, Yorkshire LS10 2QW. For brass strips, rods, and wire.

◇ FINISHES, POLISHES AND WAXES ◇

House of Harbru, 6 Newington Drive, Bury, Lancs BL8 2NE

Liberon Waxes, 6 Park Street, Lydd, Kent TN29 9AY

Matthews, Kettlebrook Road, Kettlebrook, Tamworth, Staffs B77 1AG

John Myland Ltd, 80 Norwood High Street, London SE27 9NW

Poth, Hille & Co Ltd, High Street, Stratford, London E15 2QD

Weaves & Waxes, 53c Church Street, Bloxham, Banbury, Oxon OX15 4ET

◇ VENEERS, FANS, AND SHELLS ◇

Aaronson (Veneers) Ltd, 45 Redchurch Street, London E2 7DJ

Art Veneers Co Ltd, Industrial Estate, Mildenhall, Suffolk IP28 7AY

John Boddy Timber, Riverside Saw Mills, Boroughbridge, Yorkshire YO5 9NJ

C B Veneers Ltd, River Pinn Works, Yiewsley High Street, West Drayton, Middx UB7 7TA

General Woodwork Supplies, 76–80 Stoke Newington High Street, London N16 5BR

Robbins Ltd, Merrywood Mills, Bedminster, Bristol, Avon BS3 1DX

S. Rockwood, 13–15 Seel Street, The Courtyard, Liverpool L1 4AU

Weaves & Waxes, 53c Church Street, Bloxham, Banbury, Oxon OX15 4ET

◇ GILDING MATERIALS ◇

Liberon Waxes, 6 Park Street, Lydd, Kent TN29 9AY

E. Ploton (Sundries) Ltd, 273 Archway Road, London N6 5AA

Stuart Stevenson, 66 Roding Road, London E5 0DW

G. M. Whiley Ltd, The Runway, Station Approach, South Ruislip, Middx MA4 6SQ

British-American Terminology

British	US	British	US
Aluminium	Aluminum	Machined timber	Stock
Caustic soda	Lye	Methylated spirit	Denatured alcohol
Coarse canvas	Burlap	Mushroom-head screw	Oval-head screw
Compass plane	Curved bottom plane	Oscillating sander	Vibrating sander
Cotton wool	Absorbent cotton	Oval nail	Finishing nail
Craft knife	Sloyd knife	Panel pin	Brad
Cramp	Clamp	Paraffin	Kerosene
Drawing pin	Thumbtack	Rebate	Rabbet
Finger or comb joint	Box corner joint	Sash cramp	Bar clamp
Flat bit	Spade bit	Sawn (converted) timber	Lumber
French polish	Cut shellac		
French spindle moulder	Shaper machine	Scotch glue	Animal glue
		Stopped joint (as in trenching or housing)	Gain joint
G-cramp	C-clamp		
Glasspaper	Sandpaper	Tenon with sloping haunch	Table-haunched tenon
Groove	Groove (along the grain), or dado (across the grain)	Trench	Dado
Halved bridle joint	Cross half-lap joint	Trestle	Sawhorse
Industrial alcohol	Alcohol	Turpentine substitute (or white spirit)	Mineral spirits
Liquid paraffin	Paraffin		
Loose tongue	Spline		

Further Reading

As far as we know there are no other books dealing with repairs to clock-cases as distinct from clock movements, and we recommend the following as general reading:

Bird, Anthony *English House Clocks* David & Charles (1981)

Brun, Arnold *The Amateur's Book of Clocks* Charles Greville & Co Ltd (1980)

Hayward, C. *Furniture Repairs* Evans Brothers Ltd (1967)

Hayward, C. and Wheeler, W. *Practical Woodcarving and Gilding* Evans Brothers Ltd (1973)

Lincoln, William *The Art and Practice of Marquetry* Thames & Hudson (1971)

O'Neil, Isabel *The Art of the Painted Finish for Furniture and Decoration* Wm Morrow & Co Inc (New York 1971)

Index